Furniture 2

THE SMITHSONIAN ILLUSTRATED LIBRARY OF ANTIQUES

General Editor: Brenda Gilchrist

Furniture 2

NEOCLASSIC TO THE PRESENT

William C. Ketchum, Jr.

COOPER-HEWITT MUSEUM

The Smithsonian Institution's National Museum of Design

ENDPAPERS
An advertisement by M. Dufet for the decorating firm of Chez Fernande Cabanel, 1922. Adapted from *The Decorative Twenties* by Martin Battersby (New York: Walker and Co., 1969)

FRONTISPIECE
Moorish smoking room from the John D. Rockefeller House at 4 West Fifty-fourth Street in New York City, c. 1885. The paneling and the tables are of ebonized wood. Brooklyn Museum, gift of John D. Rockefeller, Jr., and John D. Rockefeller 3rd

Art Direction, Design: JOSEPH B. DEL VALLE

Contents

1 Introduction

Volume 1 of this two-part series, *Prehistoric Through Rococo*, dealt with furniture made up to 1800. During this vast span of time surprisingly few innovations in technique and materials appeared, though many different design types emerged. Volume 2, *Neoclassic to the Present*, deals with a much shorter period, but one in which a virtual revolution in technique and taste took place.

The great bulk of household furnishings in 1750 as in 750 or even 750 B.C. were made entirely with hand tools, in limited quantity and of metal or natural materials such as wood, plant fiber and stone. They were constructed by specialists trained in a craft tradition hundreds of years old and so uniform in its application that a cabinetmaker who worked for the pharaohs could, if suddenly materialized in the seventeenth century, not only understand the duties of his latter-day counterparts but even recognize some of their tools.

However, all this was not destined to last. In the late eighteenth century a process of change set in that was to greatly alter the way in which furniture was made, who was to own it and how they were to perceive it. The basic causes for these far-reaching modifications were industrialization and population expansion.

By the mid-1700s, England had begun to develop labor-saving devices that enabled workers, assembled in large buildings or groups of buildings that came to be called factories, to produce quantities of more or less identical goods at a fraction of what it would have previously cost to turn out the same items in a scattered or "cottage" industry. In the world of furniture such innovations included, by the early 1800s, mechanical veneer saws that could cut paper-thin strips of rich woods to cover cheap pine carcasses with a thin layer of opulence, semiautomatic machines to shape nails, turning lathes to produce uniform legs and spindles and carving machinery that could imitate, albeit rather poorly, the efforts of a highly skilled woodcarver.

Colorplate 1.
Study from the Worgelt apartment on Park Avenue, New York City, 1928–30. Made in Paris and assembled in New York, the furniture and the marquetry wall panel, which were designed by Henri Redard and executed by Jean Dunand, reflect French Art Deco design at its height. The paneling used throughout the room is of palisander and olive wood. Brooklyn Museum, gift of Mr. and Mrs. Raymond Worgelt

But without a market, there would have been little purpose to such devices: the other vital element in the growth of the modern furniture industry was the development of a large group of recently urbanized middle-class consumers able to afford furniture. In the first instance, the population of Western Europe began to increase sharply in the 1700s as improved methods of agriculture provided more food and as more sophisticated techniques in sanitation and health care reduced the death rate. Further, the development of the colonial system offered a growing market for manufactured goods; and, perhaps most important, the factory workers who assembled in towns about their places of work needed furnishings and could to some extent afford them. As a result of all this, furniture manufacturers were able, for the first time, to produce for a mass market.

Of course, like most new things, this innovation had its drawbacks. During the early 1800s style was generally uniform, dictated for the most part by Napoleon, whose Empire mode was consistent if somewhat tedious. But the fall of Napoleon's house of cards led to the rise of the English manufacturers, who catered during much of the Victorian era to a public that sought and preferred revivals of prior styles. At the same time, though craftsmanship was not abandoned, there was some decline in quality.

Soon after 1850, however, new voices came to be heard. Some of these—the members of the English Arts and Crafts movement, and its European and American counterparts—argued that the only way to purge furniture design of the shoddiness and bad taste they saw in Victorian efforts was to return to a halcyon period of handcrafting located somewhere back in the fourteenth century. While the contributions of such reformers cannot be doubted, there were others who argued that industrialization and the machine were here to stay and that wise designers would take what the new technology had to offer. In time, the latter opinion prevailed.

These first proponents of factory manufacture and handcraft quality were widely separated, some in Scotland and England, others in Belgium and France, and the most influential group in Germany and Austria. As a result of this dispersion and of the resistance of more traditional designers, it was not until the turn of this century that they were able to establish themselves as a force in furniture design.

In the early 1900s their efforts began to have some effect. New materials, previously regarded as fit only for industrial use—tubular steel, chrome, aluminum, canvas and Bakelite—were added to those traditionally employed in furniture making. Their detractors said that they were ugly. Their originators argued that they were the substances of the modern age and therefore appropriate; and that, even more important, their simplicity and flexibility provided the uniformity necessary for machine production.

This, perhaps, is the key to these new designers and their mode, one that recognized no cultural or national boundaries and has become known as the International style. Unlike their Victorian predecessors, who were attempting to adapt handcrafted designs to machine production, these people were designing specifically for the machine. As a result, decoration that was both expensive and difficult to produce mechanically became, perhaps for the first time in history, subservient to line or total form.

The modern designers saw their furniture and its role in a new light. Their furnishings were not so much intended to "decorate" rooms in the traditional manner as to function in them and to be both practical and comfortable. This implied a direct relationship between furniture and the building in which it was housed. Accordingly, most twentieth-century designers have also been architects.

Furthermore, these architect–interior decorators have had to become scientists in order to deal with the vast quantities of synthetic materials (from plastic and Orlon to fiberglass) now available for furniture construction, and have had to become urban planners in order to understand and provide for the furnishing needs of an ever more urbanized and transient population. The end of their efforts is far from being in sight, but it is clear that the roles of both designer and manufacturer in modern society have little relationship to those of their forebears.

2 Empire: The Neoclassic Reformation

The nineteenth century was greeted with apprehension throughout Europe. All but the most obtuse were aware that this would be a century of change; indeed, the changes had already begun to take place. France, the Continent's perennial arbiter of style and taste, had been periodically convulsed by civil war since 1789, and now had a new and ominous leader, Napoleon I, who had usurped the powers of the ruling Directoire in November of 1799 and become established as Consul, an ancient title that did little to disguise his military dictatorship. England had lost her most important colony in the American Revolution of 1775–83 and now faced the threat of French expansionism, while Austria, Prussia and Italy were already fighting for their national lives against the seemingly invincible armies of the new Caesar.

It seemed scarcely a time for concern with such mundane subjects as furniture and decoration; and yet, for most furniture designers and manufacturers, business could continue as usual. The political and economic war between England and France had, in the preceding quarter century, been anticipated by a war of taste as designers in the two nations wrestled over the "correct" interpretation of the ancient forms of furniture and decoration uncovered during the excavations at the Italian sites of Herculaneum and Pompeii (see *Furniture 1*).

For some years the English, who favored a style based on the decorations found on Greek and Roman examples rather than on the form of these objects as preferred by the French, held the upper hand. But this "golden age" of English furniture construction could not be maintained. Even before his death, its greatest designer, Robert Adam (1728–1792), had been in partial eclipse. This state of affairs could be traced initially to the straitened economic conditions imposed on the British Isles by expenses incident to the American Revolutionary War, but it was due in larger part to the withdrawal of

Colorplate 2.
Desk-and-bookcase, mahogany, satinwood and *verre églomisé*. The design for this piece is taken from plate 38, "Sister's Cylinder Bookcase," in Thomas Sheraton's *Cabinet Dictionary* of 1803, and reflects the strong English influence on American styles of the period. American, c. 1811. Metropolitan Museum of Art, New York, gifts of Mrs. Russell Sage and various other donors, 1969

1

2

1.
Combination library table and ladder in the Sheraton style, mahogany with brass fittings (two views). Mechanical, multipurpose furnishings of the late eighteenth century were necessitated by a decrease in size of the average living space as population rose and became more centralized, but they also reflected the era's fascination with new technology. English, late eighteenth century. Cooper-Hewitt Museum, anonymous gift

2.
Pembroke table in the Sheraton style, mahogany with sycamore inlay. English, 1775–1800. Metropolitan Museum of Art, New York, gift of Mrs. Russell Sage, 1909

official commissions following the coming of age in 1783 of the Prince of Wales, an outspoken and enthusiastic Francophile. The prince had redone his official residence, Carlton House, in the French manner, and after the fall of the Bastille in 1789 he had welcomed the influx of French craftsmen and émigrés bringing French furniture. By 1800, light and elegant Adam-style furnishings were being replaced with lower, rectangular pieces featuring the broad, flat surfaces now favored in France. This style, which we know as Regency (in honor of the prince, who held the office of Regent for nine years before he became king in 1820), was dominant in England until the 1830s.

Yet the influence of such well-known British furniture designers as George Hepplewhite (d. 1786) and Thomas Sheraton (1751–1806) remained strong well into the nineteenth century. Sheraton proved particularly durable, in part because his *Cabinet-Maker and Upholsterer's Drawing-Book* (1791–94) offered designs that bridged the gap between the purely English Adam-Hepplewhite style and the French-inspired furniture of the Regency period. Sheraton's designs were practical as well as beautiful. In a period when the rapidly expanding population of the British Isles was finding housing in short supply, he created a variety of multipurpose furniture admirably suited for crowded houses and flats (plates 1 and 2).

This English version of what has become known as the early Neoclassic (to distinguish it from the later Empire) style was also adopted with enthusiasm in the former colonies, where Americans found their cultural shackles more difficult to loosen than the economic and political ones. Sophisticated cabinetmakers such as John (c. 1738–1818) and Thomas (1771–1848) Seymour of Boston, Massachusetts, toned down the form and decoration of the English originals—a typical American response—but did not hesitate to employ the rich veneers, fluting and even some of the gilt bronze favored by the English craftsmen (plate 3). Pieces of less opulence but comparable skill were produced by many other city cabinetmakers, such as Michael Allison (at work 1800–45) of New York (plate 4).

At its best, American Federal furniture (as the early Neoclassic was known in the United States) could be extremely appealing. Clean lines and slim, delicate legs caused some pieces to almost "float" above the floor; while the skilled employment of inlay and veneer in contrasting light and dark woods was very effective (plate 5 and colorplate 2). Where embellishment was required, the inlaid bellflower and swag-and-tassel festooning adapted from the English Neoclassic was accompanied by carefully controlled amounts of gilt bronze, usually limited to cabinetry hardware or the finials surmounting highboys.

The Neoclassic proved most enduring in rural areas of the new United States, such as northern New England. While cabinetmakers in coastal cities and bigger inland communities followed the shifting

3

4

3.
Sideboard, mahogany and mahogany veneer with gilt-bronze mountings, attributed to John and Thomas Seymour of Boston. American, c. 1805–10. Toledo Museum of Art, Toledo, Ohio, gift of Mr. and Mrs. George P. MacNichol, Jr.

4.
Chest of drawers, mahogany with satinwood inlay. This simple but stylish piece is the work of the cabinetmaker Michael Allison of New York. American, 1800–1810. Metropolitan Museum of Art, New York, Sylmaris Collection, gift of George Coe Graves, 1931

5.
Sideboard, mahogany with ebony, boxwood, satinwood inlay, silver and glass panels. The tambour-front knife boxes atop this sideboard are rather uncommon in American pieces. American, 1795–1800. Metropolitan Museum of Art, New York, gift of Mitchell Taradash and Pulitzer Fund, 1945

5

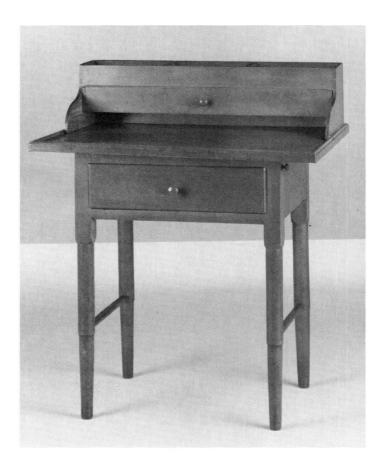

6.
Desk or sewing stand, birch. Created by the
Church family of New Lebanon, New York,
this piece incorporates the simplified Shera-
ton-style leg found on so much Shaker
furniture. American, mid-nineteenth century. Metropolitan Museum of Art, New
York, Friends of the American Wing Fund,
1966

styles of the nineteenth century, a large number of country furniture
makers continued to turn out Neoclassic pieces until after 1850. Perhaps the finest of this work was done by the Shakers, members of a
religious sect based primarily in the northeastern states. Stripping
the Neoclassic of all unnecessary decoration and refining its form,
they created chairs, tables and cupboards that seem startlingly contemporary today (plates 6 and 7).

English influence was also felt in what is now Germany, where
the foremost exponent of the early Neoclassic, David Roentgen
(1743–1807) of Neuwied, near Coblenz, termed himself an "English
Cabinet-maker," though in fact he did most of his work for the court
of Louis XVI. Roentgen, like Sheraton, was an exponent of multipurpose, mechanical furniture (colorplate 3); he created such things
as chests with secret compartments and a desk that incorporated a
music box and a clock. Roentgen's designs set the standard for German furniture until they were supplanted by Napoleonic direction
during the first decade of the nineteenth century.

Indeed, the arrival on the scene of Napoleon Bonaparte had a
profound effect on furniture design throughout the Western world.
Prior to his seizure of power in 1799, France had endured ten years of

intense instability. During that time various groups had attempted to govern the country under several different constitutions, and the results had been generally disastrous, with war, massacre and famine sweeping the country.

The Directoire, a five-member executive body established under the Constitution of 1795, had restored order to some extent, making it possible for tradesmen and artisans to go about their business with a reasonable degree of confidence. Those furniture designers who had not fled the country were again able to resume work. The attitudes of the Directoire toward furniture and its designers were basically laissez-faire—a distinct improvement over some of the earlier regimes, which had included members who saw fine furnishings as a symbol of the hated royalty and hence fit only to be destroyed.

What has become known as the Directoire, or Directory, style was of brief duration, since its promoters held office for only five years; in essence, it was little more than a somewhat simplified continuation of the early Neoclassicism prevalent during the reign of the deposed and executed Louis XVI. There was less gilt bronze, and native fruit-woods were sometimes substituted for mahogany and other rare imports (a not unreasonable concession in a time when many were homeless and destitute). Republican symbols such as the Liberty Cap, pikes and arrows replaced the iconography of the hated monarchy as furniture decoration.

Although it passed from the scene rather quickly, Directoire left a lasting impression on Europe—and on America as well. Its emphasis on archaeologically correct reproductions of Greek and Roman forms heralded the coming of Empire and hastened the transformation of English Neoclassicism to Regency. In the United States, at a somewhat later date, major designers such as Duncan Phyfe (1768–1854)

7.
Bench, pine. This strikingly up-to-date piece of furniture was used in the community dining room of the Shaker settlement at Hancock, Massachusetts. American, mid-nineteenth century. Metropolitan Museum of Art, New York, Friends of the American Wing Fund, 1966

and Charles-Honoré Lannuier (1779–1819) found a ready market for furniture in this mode.

The era of the Directory also saw the rise of two architect-designers, Charles Percier (1764–1838) and Pierre-F.-L. Fontaine (1762–1853), who were destined to establish the style for the entire Empire period. These men shared characteristics that appealed strongly to Napoleon, and when he took power in France the future of design was entrusted to their care. In the first place, like the Consul, they were practical men. As architects, they shared Adam's belief in the need for furniture to be both functional and related to the room in which it was to be used. Also, like the would-be emperor, they saw a parallel between France and ancient Rome—a course of Empire. And for the new empire, what could be more suitable than furnishings in a style duplicating as nearly as possible those of the old?

Accordingly, one of Napoleon's first acts following his self-appointment as head of state was to commission Percier and Fontaine to restore the royal palaces that had been ravaged during the preceding period of unrest. The prestige the two architects gained through this work was soon further enhanced by their publication in 1801 of the *Recueil de décorations intérieures*, a weighty tome on furniture design that firmly established the primacy in France—and eventually in all Europe—of the Empire style.

What these designers sought and largely achieved was purely classical furniture, with severely rectilinear shapes, straight lines and wide, flat, unadorned surfaces. Inlay was permitted; but for the most part the eye was focused on the rich grain of mahogany, rosewood and other exotic timbers. Not that decoration was lacking. Gilt bronze was used in profusion, alike for cabinetry hardware and the popular lion's-paw feet as well as for applied ornamentation (plate 8). The latter was found in great variety. Ancient Greek and Roman military symbols such as weapons and crowns were common, but so were lion heads, eagles and swans, and many types of floral embellishment. This was truly furniture fit for an emperor (plates 9 and 10); and in some cases appropriately enough it even bore the emperor's initial (plate 11).

As Napoleon's favorites, it fell to Percier and Fontaine to put their theories into practice. In 1804, when Napoleon tired of being Life Consul (a title awarded him two years previously) and decided to assume the title of Emperor, it was they who designed his coronation throne. Percier's work, in particular, was much sought after (colorplate 4), and his popularity and influence survived Napoleon's final defeat in 1815.

Much of the furniture designed by these two architects was actually executed by François-Honoré-Georges Jacob-Desmalter (1770–1841) and Georges II Jacob (1768–1803); brothers and cabinetmakers, they worked together until 1803 as the firm of Jacob Frères. Em-

Colorplate 3.
Architect's table, mahogany with leather and gilt-bronze mounts. This adjustable table was designed in Neuwied, Germany, by David Roentgen, a Continental exponent of the Neoclassic style. German, 1780–95. Cooper-Hewitt Museum, anonymous gift

Colorplate 4.
Cabinet for storage of medals, mahogany with applied and inlaid silver mounts. This piece was designed by Napoleon's favorite designer, Charles Percier, after an original design by Dominique Vivant Denon (1747–1825), and probably executed by the cabinetmaker François-Honoré-Georges Jacob-Desmalter. French, c. 1805. Metropolitan Museum of Art, New York, bequest of Collis P. Huntington, 1926

COLORPLATE 3

COLORPLATE 4

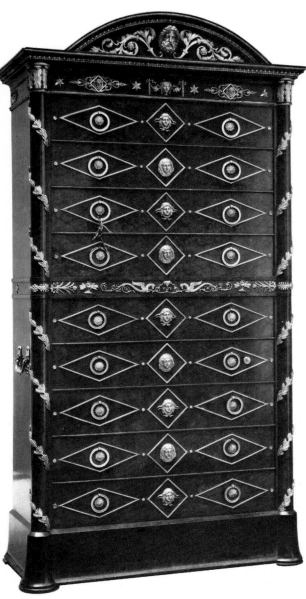

8.
Secretary-desk in the Empire style, amboyna wood with gilt-bronze mounts. Note the lavish use of gilt bronze, particularly the classical heads that grace the drawer fronts. French, 1804–15. Metropolitan Museum of Art, New York, Rogers Fund, 1923

9.
Commode, oak veneered with thuya wood, gilt-bronze mounts and marble top. Rectilinear shapes, broad flat surfaces and abundant gilt-bronze ornamentation characterized Empire furnishings. French, early nineteenth century. Metropolitan Museum of Art, New York, Rogers Fund, 1919

8

9

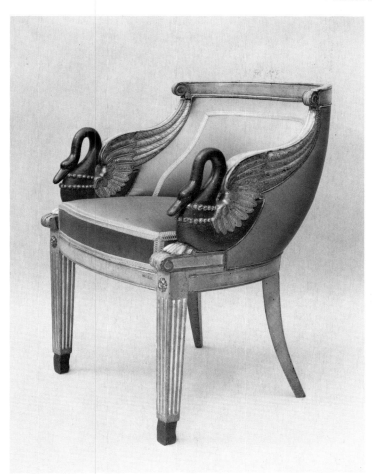

10

10.
Armchair, gilded and ebonized wood. The empress Josephine's fondness for swans led to incorporation of the bird into various furniture forms. French, c. 1805. Metropolitan Museum of Art, New York, gift of Captain and Mrs. William G. Fitch, in memory of Clyde Fitch, 1910

11.
Pair of side chairs, mahogany. Upholstered in Beauvais tapestry and bearing the imperial *N*, the chairs were once owned by the emperor Napoleon I. French, early nineteenth century. Metropolitan Museum of Art, New York; gift and bequest of Mrs. Sophie E. Minton, 1899 and 1902

11

12

13

12.
Daybed (*lit de repos*), mahogany and mahogany veneer on beech with gilt-bronze mounts. This piece was constructed in the shops of Jacob Frères. French, 1795–1803. Metropolitan Museum of Art, New York, gift of Mr. and Mrs. Charles Wrightsman, 1971

13.
Window seat, gilded walnut and chestnut, in the Empire style. Italian designers adopted this French style with enthusiasm. Italian, c. 1810. Metropolitan Museum of Art, New York, gift of Madame Lilliana Teruzzi, 1969

14.
Armchair, carved wood with leather seat and brass tacks. Long after the fall of Napoleon, Italian designers continued to work in the popular Empire style. Italian, c. 1830. Metropolitan Museum of Art, New York, Rogers Fund, 1908

15.
Table, polychromed and gilded wood, marble top. The French invasion of Egypt led to an international craze for design and decoration in the Egyptian mode. Italian, early nineteenth century. Metropolitan Museum of Art, New York, gift of Robert Lehman, 1941

ploying the finest craftsmen and using only the best materials, they established themselves as the leading furniture manufacturers of the period (plate 12 and colorplate 4). Their preference for strong, bright coverings and thick upholstery helped set the tone for the Empire style throughout Europe.

As the French armies swept across the Continent, they brought with them all the trappings of Napoleon's Empire, including its furniture, for designers in subjugated lands were quick to see the benefits of adopting the style of their conqueror. Italy in particular was an enthusiastic recipient of the new culture. Italian manufacturers were working in the Directoire style as early as 1800, adding exuberantly carved lyres, scrolls and swans to the basic Neoclassic importation. Empire found even greater favor there than in France, and remained popular for years (plates 13–15). Though Italian pieces tended to be more heavily decorated, they were faithful to the massive, rectangular forms of French Empire (plate 13), and even aped its more esoteric offshoots such as the Egyptian mode, which had a flurry of favor following Napoleon's seizure of the Nile delta in 1798 (plate 15).

Actually, the Egyptian manner is a good example of the tendency of Empire designers to attempt to swallow the classic period whole. Where the early neoclassicists of the Louis XVI–Adam camp modified ancient forms to suit their own purposes (a position generally maintained during the Directoire), Napoleon's furniture makers sought exact reproduction of historic types, or if (as was often the case) these were not available, the creation of functional hybrids. Thus examples in the Egyptian mode (plate 15) would be reproduced exactly—right

14

15

16.
Fall-front desk in the Biedermeier style, walnut and walnut veneer. Simplicity and use of native woods characterized the German version of the Empire mode. German, c. 1815–30. Private collection

17.
Daybed, polychromed sycamore, upholstered. English, early nineteenth century. Metropolitan Museum of Art, New York, Fletcher Fund, 1929

18.
Table with book-carrier, rosewood with gilt-bronze mounts. Though Regency in period, this piece reflects the innate English conservatism in its practicality and plain lines. The overall form is reminiscent of Sheraton. English, early nineteenth century. Metropolitan Museum of Art, New York, Rogers Fund, 1923

19.
Armchair, carved mahogany with leopard-skin seat. The rich carving and leopard-skin seat of this Regency chair are distinctly Continental and indicate the extent to which the French taste affected certain English cabinetmakers. English, c. 1811–20. Metropolitan Museum of Art, New York, Rogers Fund, 1967

down to the hieroglyphics which, of course, meant nothing to the owner of the furniture.

In the German states the invaders eventually drove out the last vestiges of English Sheraton-Hepplewhite design, and by 1815 local manufacturers had created a simplified, almost folk style of Empire fondly known as Biedermeier after a somewhat stodgy, comic fictional character of the period named Papa Biedermeier. This German version of Empire mimicked the straight lines and expanses of flat surface found in the high style, but economized with painting to imitate gilt bronze and carving, and employed a variety of local woods such as walnut, maple and pear in place of the more expensive mahogany (plate 16). In Germany, as in Italy, the local versions of the Empire style proved so popular that they remained in fashion for decades after Napoleon had fallen from power.

English resistance to the Empire mode was better formulated and more persistent; after all, Britain and France were at war for the greater part of the period. On the other hand, the Continental style had a strong ally in the Prince of Wales. But Directoire was more compatible with English tastes, and even as late as 1805 pieces made in the British Isles had a distinctly early Neoclassic look (colorplate 5 and plate 17). The newer style did find one powerful ally in the articulate and persuasive Thomas Hope (1769–1831), a wealthy scholar and friend of Percier. Hope's travels in Italy, Greece and Egypt led him to accept the importance of preserving "classical purity" as upheld by the leading French designers. When, in 1807, he published his design book *Household Furniture and Interior Decoration*, he provided a body of doctrine for the new believers.

English Regency furniture never approached the opulence of French Empire. It did, however, conform to the traditional dictum that mandated boxy shapes and a low profile (plates 18 and 19), and the rococo curve was definitely out. Still, practical considerations limited the amount and type of decoration employed. In a wartime economy there were few craftsmen available to perform the expensive and time-consuming tasks of marquetry work and carving (in the Empire manner carving was primarily confined to pedestals, legs and feet, anyway). Brass was often substituted for gilt bronze and inlay confined to narrow bands of contrasting wood called *stringing*, while paint might be used to hide the presumed defects of native woods.

Regency furniture types—Grecian couches, sewing tables (plate 20), circular tables with a single massive central support (monopodium) and the Trafalgar chair (an English invention based on the Greek *klismos* chair and named in honor of Admiral Nelson's triumph over the French fleet in 1805)—proved extremely popular not only with the wealthy but with the growing middle class. For the latter, there were also the less expensive and more eclectic designs, drawing on Sheraton and Directoire forms as well as on Regency, set forth in

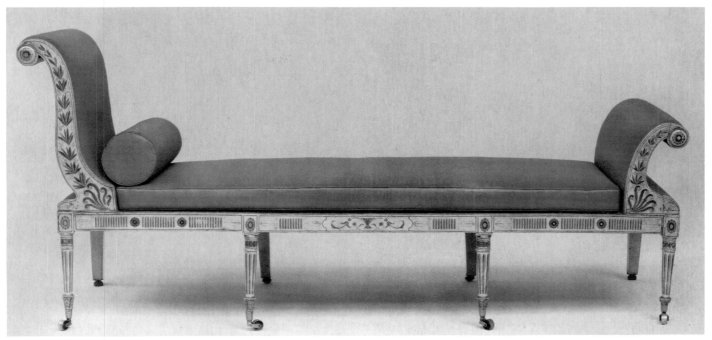

17

18

19

COLORPLATE 5

COLORPLATE 6

George Smith's *A Collection of Designs for Household Furniture and Interior Decoration* (1808). Smith was a cabinetmaker, and his examples, if less sophisticated than Hope's, were more practical and more suitable for production in quantity. Their impact on both the English and the American markets was considerable.

The Regency style predominated in England and her dependencies until well into the 1830s, and had substantial effect on other areas as well. In Italy, English Regency versions of the Empire shared popularity with the French mode after 1815, and in the United States, native variations of the Trafalgar chair were being manufactured as late as 1820, over a decade after the type had first appeared in the British Isles (plate 21).

The various manifestations of the Empire style arrived in the United States at a particularly opportune time. Business was booming following the conclusion of the War of 1812, and there was both money to spend and a renewed interest in everything European. French émigrés like Charles-Honoré Lannuier sought a haven from the uncertainties that continued to trouble their country, and from the British Isles came designers, such as Duncan Phyfe, trained in the Regency style. Together these parallel and sometimes conflicting currents fed the great stream of American Empire.

Phyfe, an immigrant from Scotland, worked in Albany prior to his arrival in New York City soon after 1790. His shop continued in New York until 1846, and he is regarded as one of the most important craftsmen of the period. Though he spent most of his life in the New World, Phyfe was never isolated from the mainstream of design. His early creations were credible examples of the Adam-Hepplewhite style, but his work during the first decade of the nineteenth century showed Sheraton and Directoire influences, and after 1810 he adopted the Regency manner (plate 22).

Duncan Phyfe furniture was generally made from mahogany or satinwood, richly carved and embellished with brass or gilt-bronze mounts, particularly after 1820 when his work took on the heavier moldings and more massive style of the Empire (colorplate 6). Especially characteristic of his pieces are the lyre-shaped forms that appear as table bases and chair backs.

The distinctly French influence on American Empire was best represented by the work of Lannuier, who came directly from Paris to New York in 1803, bringing with him the most current interpretation of the new Percier-Fontaine style. Lannuier's furniture was more elaborately carved than Phyfe's and richly mounted in gilt bronze. He preferred the exotic woods—mahogany, rosewood and satinwood—but was known to work also in native timbers such as maple. Like most manufacturers of the time, he used black paint to imitate ebony.

20.
Sewing and writing table, mahogany, cherry, rosewood, satinwood and oak, with brass and leather fittings. This lavish piece is more decorative than most English Regency examples. The globelike body opens to reveal storage areas and work surface. English, 1810–15. Metropolitan Museum of Art, New York, gift of Mrs. Paul G. Pennoyer, 1962

Colorplate 5.
Armchair, beech painted and gilded; caned seat and back. Transitional pieces such as this reflected the impact of the Empire style on the English version of the Neoclassic. English, c. 1805. Cooper-Hewitt Museum, gift of George A. Hearn

Colorplate 6.
Window seat (one of a pair), rosewood veneer, upholstered in red damask, made by Duncan Phyfe. American, c. 1825. Brooklyn Museum, gift of Mrs. J. Amory Haskell

21.
Trafalgar chair, mahogany and poplar. This side chair, made by the cabinetmaker John Hewitt (1777–1857) of New York, is based on an earlier English Regency design. American, c. 1820. Cooper-Hewitt Museum, gift of Mr. and Mrs. Norvin Hewitt Green

22.
Sofa, painted and gilded cherry. This classic example of American Empire is attributed to the workshop of Duncan Phyfe. American, c. 1815. Metropolitan Museum of Art, New York, gift of Mrs. Bayard Verplanck, 1940

Charles-Honoré Lannuier was an immediate hit among the rich and stylish, and his clientele ranged from Boston to Baltimore. His early work was in the Directoire mode, but by the time of his death in 1819, he was firmly established as an interpreter of the Empire (plate 23). Much of Lannuier's prolific output was labeled by its maker. Among the marked pieces that have been found are sleigh beds, sofas, wardrobes, chairs and tables.

Another important French-born cabinetmaker was Antoine-Gabriel Quervelle (1789–1856), who was established in Philadelphia prior to 1817. Quervelle's work in the Empire style featured mahogany, gilt metal and an occasional inlaid marble top (colorplate 7). He was well patronized by both Americans and immigrant French royalty, and was even commissioned to make furnishings for the White House. His contemporary, Michel Bouvier, was active in the same city from 1815 until 1859. He too enjoyed great patronage, including among his clients Joseph Bonaparte, brother of Napoleon.

Less well known to present-day collectors of Empire furnishings but of substantial importance in its own time was the work of Joseph Meeks & Sons. Meeks, Senior (1771–1868), was active in New York City before 1800; and his sophisticated pieces (colorplate 8) were in the best contemporary style. At a later date Meeks and his sons produced much Victorian furniture.

It should also be noted that with the exception of a few makers like Phyfe and Lannuier, American manufacturers of Empire furniture were a thrifty lot, sometimes employing paint and gilding to achieve some semblance of the luxury implied in gilt bronze and expensive woods (plates 24 and 25) but more often being content to let the

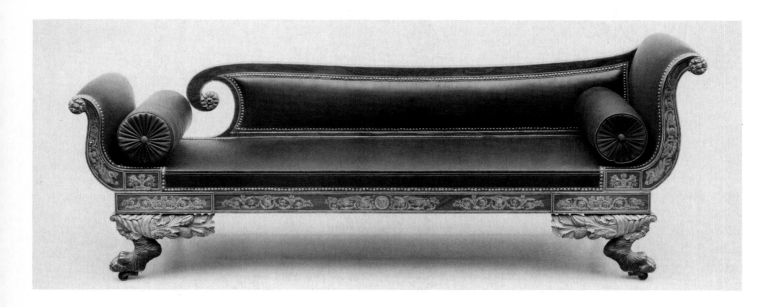

Colorplate 7.
Circular pedestal table, mahogany with gilt-brass fittings and an inlaid marble top, made by Antoine-Gabriel Quervelle of Philadelphia. American, c. 1830. Metropolitan Museum of Art, New York, Edgar J. Kaufmann Charitable Foundation Fund, 1968

23.
Card table, mahogany with gilt bronze and gilding. This piece by Charles-Honoré Lannuier of New York reflects the French influence on the American mode. Lannuier, along with Phyfe, represented the best in American Empire. American, c. 1815. Metropolitan Museum of Art, New York, funds from various donors, 1966

Colorplate 8.
Secretary in the Empire style, mahogany, pine and poplar, gilded and ebonized. This piece is attributed to Joseph Meeks & Sons, a New York City firm that made much high-quality Empire and Victorian furniture. American, c. 1825. Metropolitan Museum of Art, New York, gift of Francis Hartman Markoe, 1960

25.
Mirror, wood, gilded, with applied ornament and *verre églomisé*. American, c. 1830. Metropolitan Museum of Art, New York, gift of Mrs. J. Insley Blair, 1947

24.
Side chair, carved, painted and gilded wood. American makers often substituted paint and gilding for the exotic woods and gilt bronze employed by Europeans. American, c. 1815. Metropolitan Museum of Art, New York, Rogers Fund, 1954

26.
Washstand, mahogany. This piece foreshadows later examples of the Empire style in the United States, which tended to be much plainer than the earlier ones. American, 1815–20. Metropolitan Museum of Art, New York, gift of William R. Stewart, 1917

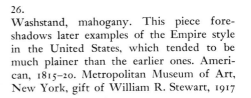

natural beauty of the wood grain speak for itself (colorplate 9 and plate 26).

Empire furnishings remained popular in the United States for a long period, coexisting peacefully with the various aspects of the Victorian. Even after 1900, furniture factories in the East and Midwest were turning out mass-produced versions of the mode. Constructed of walnut or stained hardwood, these were severely plain and bore little resemblance to the high-style pieces of the early nineteenth century.

Colorplate 9.
Settee, carved mahogany. The lines and well-balanced carving of this piece indicate it was produced by a qualified craftsman, though, like most American manufacturers of the period, he eschewed the lavish gilt-bronze ornamentation characteristic of European Empire furnishings. American, 1825–35. Cooper-Hewitt Museum

3 The Eclectic Victorians

It is perhaps appropriate that the English who had brought down Napoleon at Waterloo inherited to a substantial extent his role of design arbiter. For with the collapse of Napoleon's Empire, its furniture too passed away, to be replaced with furnishings based on a variety of earlier styles and strongly influenced in their construction and design by the effects of industrialization—a phenomenon that had originated primarily in the British Isles.

In France, Louis XVIII, a brother of the ill-fated Louis XVI, was installed on the throne in 1814; but the return of the Bourbons brought little new in the way of furniture design. Charles Percier, who was to prove far more durable than his former master, continued in the forefront—now as royal architect, a position he continued to hold during the reigns of Charles X (1824–30) and Louis Philippe (1830–48). However, Percier's well of creativity seems to have run dry. He could offer the new rulers nothing more than a succession of stylistic revivals, the first of which, Restoration, was essentially the old Directoire mode sliding gradually backward into the period of Louis XVI (plates 27–29).

This was followed in the late 1830s by a revival of the rococo known as the Louis Philippe style. It meant, of course, a return to the curve; but not in the true manner of the eighteenth century. Elements associated with the furniture of both Louis XIV and Louis XV were freely combined, and an increasing emphasis on upholstery and applied ornament led to balloonlike forms never anticipated in the earlier era.

During the 1840s interest in things medieval prompted the development of a pseudo-Gothic mode known as Troubadour, soon to be followed by a Renaissance revival (plate 30) that reached its height during Napoleon III's Second Empire (1852–71). Thereafter there was periodic interest in classic, Oriental and Near Eastern themes

Colorplate 10.
Cabinet in the Renaissance revival style, rosewood with gilt-bronze mounts and applied porcelain plaques. By Alexander Roux (at work 1837–81) of New York, this piece reflects the French influence on American taste. American, 1866. Metropolitan Museum of Art, New York, Edgar J. Kaufmann Charitable Foundation Fund, 1968

27

28

27.
Armchair in the Restoration style, mahogany and mahogany veneer over oak and poplar. In contrast to the preceding period, simplicity of line and less gilt bronze generally characterized Restoration period furnishings. French, c. 1830. Cooper-Hewitt Museum, bequest of Mrs. John Innes Kane

28.
Dressing table, mahogany with marble top and gilt-bronze mounts. French, 1815-30. Metropolitan Museum of Art, New York, gift of Mrs. Frederick S. Lee, 1922

29.
Cabinet, oak, tulipwood and marble, inlaid with Sèvres plaques in porcelain and mounted in gilt bronze. French, c. 1822. Metropolitan Museum of Art, New York, gift of Samuel H. Kress Foundation, 1958

30.
Cabinet, ebony, ebonized wood and ivory inlay, labeled Soubrier. Though generally Renaissance revival in style, like many pieces of the time this cabinet reflects a variety of influences. French, c. 1870–80. Cooper-Hewitt Museum, gift of Howard Wise

COLORPLATE 11

COLORPLATE 12

(colorplate 11), but nothing really new emerged from France until the rise of Art Nouveau in the 1880s.

One should not, incidentally, assume that the above-mentioned styles were mutually exclusive. In France, as in other countries during the mid-nineteenth century, it was common for several different modes to exist simultaneously; indeed, it was not at all unusual for the same piece to reflect influences from several different styles (plate 30).

Although developments in France during the period 1815–85 are of importance to an understanding of the Victorian mode, furniture of this style reached its greatest heights and excesses across the Channel. The name of England's Queen Victoria (reigned 1837–1901) has been given to the entire era, although manifestations of the Victorian appeared as early as 1830 and lingered until the start of World War I.

That Victorian furnishings should have been developed most fully in the British Isles is a reflection of the unique economic and social conditions existing there during the period. England entered the industrial era earlier than any other European nation. The establishment of a national railway system in the 1830s, coupled with expansion of England's overseas markets, led to the development of large industrial cities. The people who flocked to work in these centers were the world's first factory workers; and hard though their lives were, they did have money, something most barter-oriented peasants did not. What they did not have were homes and home furnishings. The builders provided the former, and the new mass-furniture manufacturers set out to provide the latter.

However, the working class and the middle-class tradesmen and artisans wanted something in the way of furniture quite different from what most manufacturers had been accustomed to producing. The wealthy had expected designer-created, carefully handcrafted one-of-a-kind examples. These were far too expensive for most of the new consumers, so the makers had to look for ways to cut expenses and increase their output.

First, they threw out the designers and, with the aid of pattern books like Henry Whitaker's *The Practical Cabinet-Maker and Upholsterer's Treasury of Designs* (1847), they became manufacturer-designers. Then they set about producing furniture their new clients could afford. In this venture they were greatly assisted by the development of various labor-saving devices, including carving tools that allowed for the mass production of decorative pieces previously cut by hand, and veneer saws that enabled a body of cheap pine or deal to be disguised behind a thin facade of richly figured mahogany. Though the great bulk of furniture remained primarily handmade, the new, steam-driven tools greatly facilitated a form of standardized production.

This trend was further accentuated by the popularization at mid-century of cast- and wrought-metal furnishings. Most popular were

Colorplate 11.
Octagonal table in the Near Eastern manner, Chinese cloisonné enamel top, brass bells, bronze pedestal. French, late nineteenth century. Cooper-Hewitt Museum, gift of Mrs. D. Chester Noyes

Colorplate 12.
Desk, papier-mâché with paint and mother-of-pearl inlay. Made in many English factories, papier-mâché proved to be an attractive and amazingly durable substitute for rare woods. English, c. 1870. Cooper-Hewitt Museum, gift of Mrs. Rogers Denckla

inexpensive brass beds, which had been favored by many even in Sheraton's time for their hygienic value (bedbugs and other vermin could not hide in them). Cast-iron chairs, tables and settees also became available in England and the United States (plate 31), primarily as garden furniture, and improvements in heating were marked by the introduction of iron stoves and radiators (plate 32).

Another unusual material was papier-mâché (colorplate 12). This had been in use for some years, but its production was greatly expanded, particularly in the Birmingham factories, by new technical innovations. Made of pulped paper and glue built up over a wood or metal framework, papier-mâché could be molded into many forms, popular among which were tables, chairs, beds and sofas. Decoration was of the painted, floral type applied on a black or red ground with the frequent addition of inlay in mother-of-pearl. In keeping with the nineteenth-century interest in things Oriental, bamboo furniture

32

31

31.
Cast-iron garden bench. Manufactured by Peter Timmes of Brooklyn, New York, this piece is typical of the iron furnishings made in both England and the United States. American, second half of the nineteenth century. Smithsonian Institution, Office of Horticulture

32.
Radiator, cast iron, made by Stratton & Seymour of New York. This early example of decorative cast iron is strongly Neo-classic in feeling. American, first half of the nineteenth century. Cooper-Hewitt Museum, gift of Edith Wetmore

was also very much in vogue. Where the real thing was either not available or not suitable, maple and other hardwoods were turned to imitate it.

Though in some cases the materials of which these Victorian furnishings were made were innovative, the designs in which they appeared were not. With the designer and architect largely driven from the field or confined to a limited number of wealthy patrons, the manufacturers were left to their own devices, and what they (and their clients) preferred were the vestiges of past civilizations and past grandeur. As in France, free adaptations of everything from the Gothic to the rococo served to whet the new dreams of grandeur.

None of this furniture looked quite like its prototype, and this was not merely a matter of ignorance or artistic preference. It reflected a basic tenet of all Victorian design: the emphasis on comfort. The coiled inner spring had been invented in the late 1820s; this feature combined with an abundance of upholstery served to achieve a bulky, rounded profile that was quite different from anything that had been previously known.

Nevertheless, during the period between 1830 and 1851—the year of the famed Crystal Palace Exhibition, which is generally regarded as marking the end of the first phase of the Victorian era—several different styles emerged. The first of these was the Grecian, which represented the final stage in the Neoclassicism that had prevailed since the eighteenth century. Like so much Victorian furniture, the Grecian showed vast unevenness in quality. Designer-made pieces compared favorably with the best Regency examples, while mass-produced furnishings were overdecorated and had a heaviness ill suited to their classic origins.

By the middle of the 1830s the rococo had arrived on the scene, fueled by a return of English buyers to the French market. Unlike the Grecian (and other styles such as the Elizabethan and Gothic), the rococo was a real departure from the Neoclassic in that there was a basic change in form—from rectilinear to curvilinear. The cabriole leg reappeared (plate 33), as did balanced S- and C-scroll curves, and naturalistic fruit and foliage carving. However, unlike the true rococo, the revival decoration was often machine-cut and applied; and other materials such as laminated wood were employed to produce a less expensive product. Perhaps the most enduring and endearing of all rococo revival forms was the balloon-back chair, so called for a fancied resemblance to the shape of a hot-air balloon. Graceful and comfortable, the balloon back occupied a prominent place in Victorian dining rooms from 1830 until well into the seventies.

Also popular were the Elizabethan and Gothic revivals, both of which featured basically rectangular forms onto which were grafted a variety of decorative details vaguely associated with the historical periods from which they were derived. In the case of the Elizabethan,

33.
Armchair, rosewood and walnut with ivory inlay, attributed to Stephen Webb (at work 1885–97). This piece is typically Victorian in its combination of several stylistic elements, such as the cabriole leg, generally associated with the rococo, and inlay in the arabesque manner. English, c. 1885–97. Cooper-Hewitt Museum, gift of Edward J. Wormley and James Merrick Smith

Colorplate 13.
Side chairs in the Elizabethan style. Both
pieces incorporate the typical Elizabethan
spiral turnings, but the chair at left also
has the blocky shape of the Neoclassic,
while the one at right, which is gilded and
inlaid with mother-of-pearl, bears the cabriole leg associated with rococo revival.
English, c. 1860–80. Cooper-Hewitt Museum, gift of Lucy C. Stark and Jennifer
Kruger

34.
Piano and two stools in the classic revival mode. Ebony and cedar with inlay in ivory and panel painted by Sir Edward Poynter (1836–1919). Designed by the English painter Sir Lawrence Alma-Tadema (1836–1912) for an American client, c. 1884. Private collection

35.
Roundabout chair in carved walnut. Italian, Renaissance revival style, c. 1870. Cooper-Hewitt Museum, gift of Adeline F. and Caroline R. Wing

36.
Sofa and side chair, laminated and solid rosewood, veneered in part over an oak frame. Attributed to John Henry Belter, these pieces are typical of the North American rococo revival style. American, 1840–50. Cooper-Hewitt Museum, gift of Mrs. Edwin Gould

37.
Detail of crest of the side chair in plate 36 showing carving and lamination

35

these included spiral-turned chair legs and uprights and strapwork, as well as machine-produced pierced carving and applied moldings (colorplate 13). The overstuffed seats and backs of such pieces were often covered with elaborate needlework in vaguely medieval patterns. Closely related was the Gothic mode, a romantic style inspired by the architecture and furnishings of the thirteenth and fourteenth centuries as seen through the eyes of nineteenth-century poets and designers. Forms remained square or rectangular as in the Neoclassic era, while factory-shaped arches, clustered columns and tracery were added.

So great was the demand for neo-Gothic and Elizabethan pieces that in some cases furniture makers actually took fragments of earlier examples in the style (such as carved panels and moldings from the many French churches and châteaus destroyed during the Revolution) and employed them in the manufacture of furniture. These pseudo-antiques have caused problems for antiquarians and museum personnel ever since.

The Crystal Palace Exhibition of 1851 was the high point of Victorian eclecticism, providing a veritable showcase for the many products of the manufacturer-designers. Thereafter, however, trained designers began once more to emerge, and a movement toward simpler, more functional design appeared. Yet the revival styles would remain popular with most manufacturers and customers throughout the rest of the century. It was, for example, quite common to find massive classic revival furnishings (plate 34) in the most sophisticated English and American households at a time when new modes such as Art Nouveau and Arts and Crafts were already well developed.

Particularly popular in the 1860s and 1870s were furnishings in the Renaissance revival style, based on Italian furnishings of the sixteenth century. These generally rectangular pieces were heavily carved and inlaid with various materials in a manner deemed appropriate to their period. The Renaissance revival was favored not only in England and the United States but, appropriately enough, in Italy, where it proved to be one of the few revival styles to gain significant acceptance among a population that still clung doggedly to the Empire taste (plate 35).

Victorian furniture and pattern books were widely distributed throughout the Western world, and nowhere did they make a greater impact than in the United States. By the 1840s the new Republic was sufficiently prosperous and sufficiently removed from its revolutionary beginnings to welcome designs based on furniture made for royalty. All the revivals—Gothic, Renaissance, Elizabethan and so on—found their adherents; but none was so popular as the rococo, and it was in this style that the most important American cabinet-makers of the period worked.

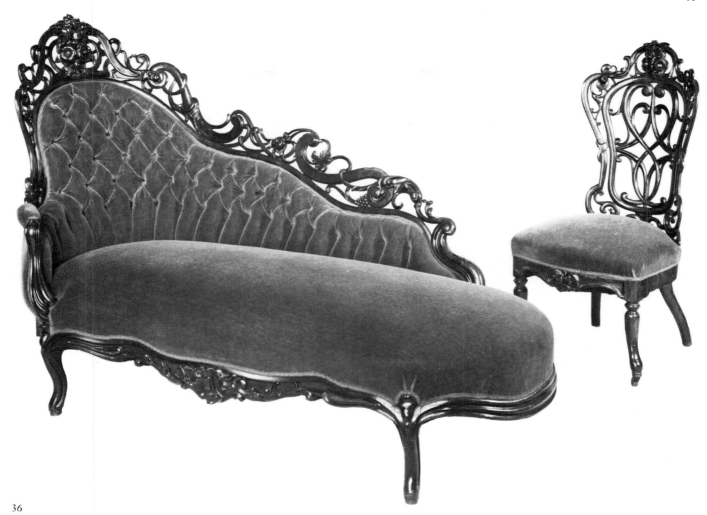

36

37

Foremost among these manufacturers was John Henry Belter (1804–1863). Born in Germany, he emigrated to the United States in the late 1830s or early 1840s and is first listed as a cabinetmaker in New York City in 1844. He remained active there until his death, and the firm was continued by his relatives by marriage, the Springmeyers, until it succumbed to bankruptcy in 1867. Belter is best known for his parlor and bedroom suites, which featured richly carved frameworks in rosewood and walnut with heavy rolled moldings and intricate fruit and floral decoration. Usually covered in fine brocades and damasks, Belter pieces were regarded as just the thing for prosperous merchants and rising young professionals (plate 36).

Belter's greatest achievement is generally considered to be his successful application of laminating to furniture manufacture. Other innovators had worked with what we now term plywood, but Belter appears to have been the first to recognize the practical advantages of this material in producing complex but durable carving. In the preface

38

39

38.
Armchair, pierced and carved rosewood, upholstered. Attributed to the firm of Joseph Meeks & Sons, this piece is in the rococo revival style. American, 1850–65. Metropolitan Museum of Art, New York, gift of Mr. and Mrs. Lowell Ross Burch and Jean McLean Marron, 1951

39.
Reclining armchair, cherry with velvet seat and back. This piece was patented February 6, 1866, by the George Hunzinger firm of New York City. American, 1866. Metropolitan Museum of Art, New York, gift of Mrs. D. Chester Noyes, 1968

to his patent application of February 23, 1858, Belter noted that "Pressed work [as he called plywood] is invariably composed entirely of veneers and glue. The grain of each veneer is laid at right angles to that of the next, and the whole being firmly and smoothly glued together, it is a very strong and durable material." Steamed and shaped to a curvilinear form under pressure, and having the strength of cross-grain construction, Belter chair and sofa backs were pierced and carved to create the effect of openwork carving in a curved plane, an effect that would have been impossible to achieve with natural wood (plate 37).

For many years nearly all nineteenth-century furnishings made in this manner were attributed to the Belter shop, despite the fact that the firm rarely seems to have labeled or otherwise marked its output, and no factory catalogues are presently known. In the 1970s researchers cautiously began crediting much Belter-type furniture to other contemporary producers, particularly to the firm of Joseph Meeks & Sons (plate 38). During the 1850s and 1860s Meeks & Sons produced substantial quantities of carved, laminated furniture in the rococo manner, much of which is generally similar in style and construction to that produced by Belter.

Lamination was just one of many technical innovations fostered by American manufacturers. They were not far behind their British cousins in the production of *patent furniture* (a term in general use though many of the pieces so called were never officially patented), the mechanical multipurpose pieces first promoted by Thomas Sheraton. Everything from reclining chairs (plate 39) to beds that sprang out of the wall or emerged from sofas poured out of the Eastern and Midwestern factories.

Perhaps one of the most interesting American innovations was the Wooton desk, a remarkable all-in-one office intended for use in business firms, railway offices and other places where there was need for a desk that combined a writing area with multiple storage and filing

40.
Wooton desk, oak and burl oak, with brass fittings. Lined with drawers and cubbyholes, the Wooton desk was a compact miniature office. American, 1874–84. Smithsonian Institution, National Museum of History and Technology

space. Made primarily in the 1870s and most often vaguely Renaissance revival in style, Wooton desks were manufactured in Indianapolis, Indiana, and sold throughout the United States (plate 40).

Another interesting American type was horn furniture. As sportsmen penetrated the vast wilderness of the Far West, they brought back trophies—everything from buffalo skulls to deer and elk horns. It became fashionable to make the horns into furniture, particularly tables and chairs (plate 41), to be used in hunting camps and other rustic summer dwellings. Such pieces had in most cases no discernible style, though they clearly owed much in conception to early nineteenth-century German lodge furniture.

But, of course, most American furniture of the period was in one of the accepted Victorian revival styles: Grecian (colorplate 14), rococo (plate 38), Gothic (plate 42) and Renaissance (see colorplate 10, page 34) were all immensely popular during the period between the Civil War and World War I. Lesser modes, such as the Egyptian revival (plate 43), had more limited appeal.

Germany lingered for years in the modified Empire manner known as Biedermeier, though brief Renaissance and Gothic revivals had some effect. However, it was in Austria that one of the most important developments of the era took place. Michael Thonet (1796–1871),

41.
Two armchairs, moose and elk antlers. Made in Wyoming, these rustic pieces are a graphic reflection of the frontier spirit. American, c. 1900. Wyoming State Archives and Historical Department, Cheyenne

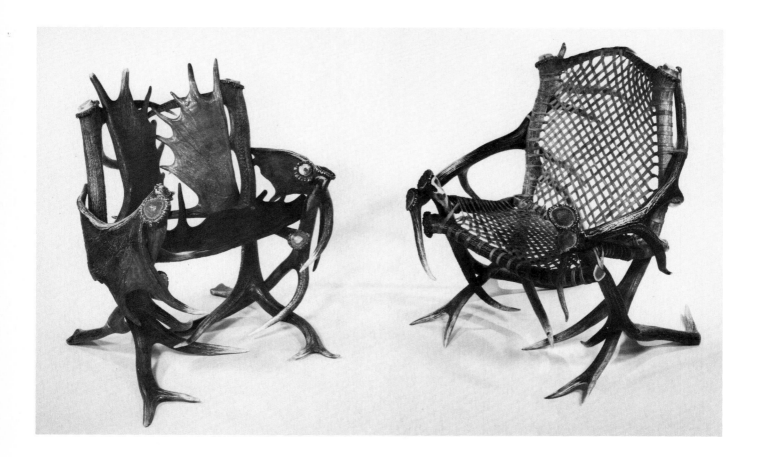

42.
Gothic revival bedstead, pierced and carved walnut. The marble-topped walnut and burl oak side table is of the same style and period. American, c. 1850, Smithsonian Institution, National Museum of History and Technology, gift of the City of Bridgeport, Connecticut

who had been born in Prussia and trained there as a cabinetmaker, established himself in Vienna in the 1840s. He first experimented with veneer making, but soon graduated to steaming and bending under pressure solid wooden rods—generally of beech, as this wood due to its unusually tight grain seemed most capable of withstanding stress when flexed.

Thonet's furniture was destined to be a great commercial success. It was extremely attractive in a vaguely rococo way, with graceful, flowing lines that seemed to presage the coming of Art Nouveau. But it was much more than that. Bentwood, as it came to be known, was the first furniture genuinely to lend itself to mass production. The struts could be steamed and bent to shape, and they would retain this shape when dry even as individual units. Moreover, these elements were so strong that they could be put together with a few screws and small metal braces rather than the costly dowels, glue and carved braces required for other furniture of the period. This made it possible

Colorplate 14.
Shelf clock in the Grecian revival style, marble, glass and gilt bronze, manufactured by P. W. Taylor of Brooklyn, New York. In the second half of the nineteenth century, the United States became the world's greatest source of mass-produced timepieces. American, 1896. Brooklyn Museum, gift of Mr. and Mrs. Samuel B. Feld

43.
Pedestal, walnut and burl walnut with poplar, marble top and gilded and polychrome decoration. Pieces in the Egyptian revival style, such as this one, are relatively uncommon in the United States. American, c. 1860–70. Metropolitan Museum of Art, New York, funds from various donors, 1970

44.
Bentwood console table by Thonet Brothers in steamed and shaped hardwood. The first "modern" furniture, bentwood was a revelation in its day and continues to be popular. Austrian, c. 1850–1900. Cooper-Hewitt Museum, purchased in memory of Erskine Hewitt

to ship unassembled pieces of bentwood furniture to any spot in the world and have them assembled there.

It was a good thing for Michael Thonet that he patented his invention, for when the bentwood creations were shown in London at the 1851 Great Exhibition they were an immediate hit. By the mid-1850s, Thonet's firm (which had been transferred to his five sons, "Gebrüder Thonet," in 1853) was the world's largest producer of factory-made furniture, with an export trade that covered all of Europe as well as North and South America. Bentwood furniture has remained popular to the present day, and the basic style has been produced by many different manufacturers; but no one has succeeded in excelling the grace and strength of the original (plate 44).

In its standardization of form, factory-type construction and relative inexpensiveness, bentwood is truly the prototype of Victorian furniture. The many styles and great quantities of furnishings produced during the period could never have existed without the technical innovations that were being developed. In any case, there would have been no need for either such quantity or variety had not the social structure of Europe and North America changed with the emergence of new groups of people needing furniture and able for the first time to afford it.

43

44

4 The Arts and Crafts Movement: Resurgence of Design

The undeniable importance of the Victorian designer-manufacturers lies in their role as providers of inexpensive and comfortable furnishings for a vast new audience: the first mass-market consumers of the industrial age. This said, there cannot be much doubt that these manufacturers, with the exception of Thonet, offered very little in the way of creative design. Moreover, their construction methods were often expedient to the point of being shoddy. It was of course inevitable that a reaction should occur. But it took many years for an important designer-based movement to make much headway against the popularity of the revivalist manner, and the early reformers met with little favor outside their own set.

One of these lonely pioneers was Augustus Welby Northmore Pugin (1812–1852), an English architect and designer of French parentage. Something of a prodigy, Pugin was designing chairs for Windsor Castle at the age of fifteen. His first efforts were in the prevailing Gothic revival style and were done in the accepted manner, that is, by applying factory-cut decoration to a basic Neoclassic frame.

Pugin was apparently not satisfied with the results, for he began to study the historical antecedents of these neo-Gothic pieces and became interested in their structure as well as their decoration. This research led him to favor handcrafted furniture (since, of course, all true Gothic furniture had been made entirely by hand) and what is termed *revealed construction*—that is, the visualization of design techniques such as peg-held joints and dovetails as important parts of an object's decorative scheme rather than as something purely functional and unsightly that should be concealed from view. Since Victorian cabinetmakers were then busily employing glue, dowels and putty to hide all signs of how their pieces had been constructed, Pugin's ideas were revolutionary.

Colorplate 15.
Easel, walnut with paint and gilding. In the Eastlake mode, this easel reflects a major pastime of middle-class Victorians: amateur pursuit of the fine arts. American, c. 1870. Brooklyn Museum, gift of the Estate of Mrs. William H. Good

His design book *Gothic Furniture in the Style of the Fifteenth Century*, published in 1835, made his theories clear. Some of them could scarcely have been to the liking of his contemporaries in the furniture world, especially his objection to mass production and his expressed contention that "the great test of beauty is the fitness of design for the purpose for which it was intended." This statement, which might well be the credo for all modern design, became the rallying cry of all later reformers who sought to relate style to function.

Though Pugin did not hesitate to put his theories into practice, particularly in creating the Medieval Court for the Crystal Palace Exposition of 1851, his goal of handcraftsmanship had little impact on the commercial furniture factories of his day, which continued to crank out their mass-produced pseudo-Gothic reproductions.

It was not until the 1860s that another important reformer appeared on the scene. William Morris (1834–1896) was not a furniture designer, being more interested in such accessories as wallpaper and textiles, but he fully shared Pugin's belief in the dignity and quality of medieval furnishings. Though a man of far-ranging intellect (he was once offered Oxford University's chair in poetry) and an important social reformer, Morris was also an extremely practical businessman. In 1861 he founded Morris, Marshall, Faulkner & Company, an interior design firm specializing in ecclesiastical furnishings. After he took sole control in 1875, this became Morris & Company, one of the great firms of the late nineteenth and early twentieth centuries.

Morris's business associate and the man who designed most of the firm's early furniture was Philip Webb (1831–1915), an architect and interior designer who favored sturdy, medieval pieces, particularly tables, benches and settles, primarily made of oak with the exposed construction championed by Pugin. At first, the more expensive examples in this style—sometimes decorated with painted panels by Morris or his friends, the painters Dante Gabriel Rossetti (1828–1882) and Edward Burne-Jones (1833–1898)—as well as the lesser pieces, which Morris dubbed "workaday" furniture, were made almost entirely by hand (plate 45). However, particularly after Webb's retirement around 1890, Morris also began to produce substantial quantities of reproduction furniture modeled on eighteenth-century styles. Though well made, these pieces were highly decorated with veneer and marquetry, and fell comfortably within the nineteenth-century tradition of revival style.

The clean lines and honest oak of the early pieces nevertheless had a profound effect on a market glutted with veneer and excessive decoration. Particularly well known among Morris-Webb products are the rush-seated, turned chairs known as the Sussex type, and the leather-upholstered armchairs with turned members and adjustable backs that came, in the United States at least, to be known as Morris chairs.

45.
Cabinet-on-stand, polychromed wood. This early Arts and Crafts–style piece was designed by Philip Webb, an associate of William Morris, and is embellished with a painted door panel by the pre-Raphaelite painter Sir Edward Burne-Jones. English, c. 1861. Metropolitan Museum of Art, New York, Rogers Fund, 1926

46.
Library cabinet, oak with brass fittings. The designer of this piece, Charles Lock Eastlake, was an early advocate of simple, practical home furnishings. English, c. 1865–70. Private collection

Colorplate 16.
Fall-front desk, ebonized maple, cherry and cedar with gilt-bronze fittings. The Eastlake mode was extremely popular in the United States. This example is by Herter Brothers of New York City, manufacturers of fine furniture from about 1865 to 1905. American, c. 1877–82. Metropolitan Museum of Art, New York, gift of Paul Martini, 1969

47.
Bedstead, cherry, ebonized, with marquetry and stencil decoration. Also made by Herter Brothers, this piece indicates the limits to which American designers took the relatively plain Eastlake style. American, c. 1880. Metropolitan Museum of Art, New York, gift of Paul Martini, 1969

Much of the best furniture produced by Morris & Company was too expensive for the average consumer and, initially at least, too far removed from the common taste to attract much attention. Yet his ideas did not fall on deaf ears. On the contrary, in the 1880s they were destined to inspire a great revival of handwork known as the Arts and Crafts movement. Ironically, those who at first applied his precepts were not artists or designers but some of those for whom he had reserved his strongest criticism, the designer-manufacturers.

Following the showing of several handmade, Gothic-inspired pieces at the 1862 London Exhibition, a number of conscientious furniture manufacturers enlisted trained designers to create pieces for them with the express purpose of producing quality mass-produced furniture. Such pieces are frequently referred to as art furniture. Some of these designers were members of a group loosely termed the Aesthetic movement, a precursor of the Arts and Crafts movement. Best known among designers of this period was Charles Lock Eastlake (1836–1906), an English architect and art historian. Eastlake was,

48

49

48.
Oak wardrobe, with brass fittings. Designed by William Burges, this piece reflects the strong emphasis on joinery in the Gothic mode favored by members of the Aesthetic movement. English, c. 1850–60. Private collection

49.
Armchair, ebonized hardwood. This piece by Edward William Godwin reflects a careful balance between traditional English country furniture forms and Oriental elements, characterized by the arms. English, c. 1870–80. Private collection

like Morris and Pugin, an advocate of simple, functional and well-constructed pieces, although his taste ran more to the Jacobean and Elizabethan modes than to the neo-Gothic style (plate 46). He had few kind words for the practices of the large manufacturers, accusing them of a "cheap and easy method of workmanship in an endeavor to produce a show of finish with the least possible labor. . . ."

But Eastlake was no Utopian. His *Hints on Household Taste*, published in 1868, advocated the use of simple, relatively undecorated furniture, which could be largely manufactured in the existing factories. Eastlake's theories were received favorably, especially among the middle classes in England and also in the United States, where a so-called Eastlake style was prevalent throughout the last quarter of the nineteenth century. Yet in the hands of the great manufacturers, such as Herter Brothers of New York, Eastlake's forms often retained little more than their basic rectangular shapes. The decoration of the pieces often became so lavish that their original advocate would have found them unrecognizable (colorplate 16 and plate 47). Basically medieval outlines were overlaid with pseudo-Oriental decorative devices, chip carving, turning, inlay, gilding and even ceramic tiles.

Other designers influential in the art furniture field were Bruce Talbert (1838–1881), whose *Gothic Forms Applied to Furniture*, first issued in 1867, became almost a bible for the commercial manufacturers of Gothic-type furniture during the 1870s, and William Burges (1827–1881). Burges, too, preferred the medieval mode (plate 48), though he was also greatly interested in Japanese design and decoration and incorporated these into some of his work. Both Talbert and Burges had important private clients for whom they worked, but they

50.
Firescreen, cherry, pierced and molded, with stained-glass panels. Turn-of-the-century American designers proved particularly adept in the use of stained glass. American, late nineteenth century. Metropolitan Museum of Art, New York, Edgar J. Kaufmann Charitable Foundation Fund, 1969

were willing to design for the commercial manufacturers. Talbert, for example, created many pieces for Holland & Sons, one of the most important late nineteenth-century English factories.

By far the most active commercial designer of the art furniture period was Edward William Godwin (1833–1886), who began creating furniture, textiles and carpets for such manufacturers as Collinson & Lock and W. A. Smee in 1868. Godwin was greatly affected by Japanese art and architecture, and the book on his work entitled *Art Furniture from Designs by E. W. Godwin, F.S.A. and Others* (1877) included many examples of what he chose to term "Anglo-Japanese" furnishings.

Godwin's furniture was characterized by an airy, rectilinear structure, showing a startlingly modern balancing of solids and voids. Decoration was varied, with the designer employing everything from carving and Japanese "leather paper" to delicate silver and ivory mounts (often against an ebonized background). In all cases, though, the decoration was modest in quantity and subservient to the form of the piece—something quite uncharacteristic of the time (plate 49).

Interesting as their work was, the compromises that the designers of art furniture inevitably had to make with the demands of commercial and even mass production were not tolerable to many of their fellows. Gradually more and more architects, designers and craftsmen turned to the teachings, if not necessarily the practice, of William Morris.

In the early 1880s these creative individuals began to gather together in small groups with the aim of combining good design with fine handcraftsmanship. The first of these organizations to emerge was the Century Guild, founded in 1882 primarily through the efforts of Arthur Heygate Mackmurdo, an architect and designer who was to prove instrumental in the development of the English version of the Art Nouveau. Other similar organizations followed in short order. There were the St. George's Art Society (1883), the Art-Workers' Guild (1884), the Guild of Handicraft (1888) and finally the Arts and Crafts Exhibition Society (also 1888), the group that eventually gave its name to the whole rather amorphous movement.

In their own way, the Arts and Crafts–oriented designers were just as eclectic as those manufacturers whose excesses they criticized. To begin with, the various organizations were made up of different workers in various mediums, not just furniture but glass, ceramics, metal, textiles and the fine arts. Everyone wanted to share in the creative process, and much of the furniture was the product of a group or cooperative effort rather than bearing the imprint of a single designer's concept. This was fine in theory—indeed, exactly what most of the membership wanted—but it did not make for a unified and clearly defined style.

Nevertheless, the movement attracted considerable attention, in substantial part the result of its periodic exhibitions, the first of which occurred in 1888. The pieces displayed proved to be of interest to a limited number of wealthy patrons as well as to a few commercial manufacturers such as the important London house of Collinson & Lock. Yet the high-quality handcraft techniques and applied artwork made most Arts and Crafts furnishings too expensive for general sale.

The first members of the movement to deal seriously with this problem were the Barnsley brothers, Ernest (1863–1926) and Sidney (1865–1926), and Ernest Gimson (1864–1919). All three were architects and designers, and Gimson was a close friend of William Morris, whose ideas greatly affected his attitude toward furniture design and craftsmanship. Gimson was particularly concerned with the difficulty of providing honestly made and artistically pleasing pieces at prices the general public could afford. To achieve this, he and the Barnsleys established a London furniture factory in 1890 under the title of Kenton & Company.

Like Morris before them, the partners encountered financial problems in creating and marketing good, inexpensive furniture in the Arts and Crafts tradition. In 1892 they were forced to close their London shop. They decided to move to the Cotswolds, a remote area in the southwest that had escaped the worst effects of the Industrial Revolution and where crafts still flourished. In 1894 they set up shop at Pinbury Park, in Gloucestershire, where Gimson directed the making of traditional ladder-back, rush-seated chairs from native woods, while the brothers designed a wide variety of furnishings.

The workshop was later (1902) reestablished at Daneway House in Sapperton, Gloucestershire, where it remained active until Gimson's death. During this period the brothers largely retired from the business (though Sidney continued to work nearby), and Gimson became the prime force. He gathered a group of highly skilled workmen, put them under the supervision of a Dutch cabinetmaker, Peter Waals (1864–1919), and devoted himself to designing.

The early work of Gimson and the Barnsleys, especially that produced in London, had been plain to the point of severity. Oak was their favorite wood, and most pieces showed broad, flat surfaces, richly grained, stiffly rectangular and devoid of any decoration other than the metal hardware. Once Gimson was on his own, though, he allowed free rein to his imagination and a complete understanding of the craft processes. He used revealed construction as a form of decoration, utilized many different woods (oak, yew, walnut and elm, often contrasting shades of timber in the same piece) and did not hesitate to employ such seemingly uncountrylike decorative elements as ebony, silver and mother-of-pearl.

Largely through the efforts of Gimson and the Barnsleys, the ideas of William Morris were substantially realized in the late nineteenth and early twentieth centuries. A growing clientele of sophisticated consumers bought their furniture and gradually forced many commercial manufacturers to make at least some effort to meet their standards. Beyond the British Isles, the movement to restore craftsmanship and to simplify furniture manufacture was on the whole well received, though sometimes with results its proponents could not have anticipated. In general the Continent showed itself quite ready to give up the succession of revivals that had dominated styles since the 1820s. This was in part a reflection of the English export trade, for the nation had become the world's largest manufacturer and distributor of factory-made furnishings. But it also mirrored the very considerable respect for the English designers that existed among the European intelligentsia.

In Austria and Germany, Godwin's art furniture was much admired; and the various associations of artisans, designers and artists that arose at the turn of the century owed much in their philosophy to the thinking of William Morris and his contemporaries. Thus the Austrian architect and designer Adolf Loos (1870–1933), in attacking what he perceived to be excesses in Art Nouveau design, urged his colleagues to "find beauty in form instead of making it rely on ornament."

Holland was particularly affected by the English reform movement. The architect K. P. D. de Bazel (1869–1923) provided a theoretical basis in the Morris tradition, while the designer Hendrik Petrus Berlage (1856–1934) carried this to fulfillment in plain, unornamented pieces that clearly owed much to Arts and Crafts design. The results in Belgium were quite different. There, the reformers' emphasis on simple, sturdy materials and honest craftsmanship was much applauded, but the work produced by the dominant Brussels School was more in the Art Nouveau manner.

In the United States it was the less complex, more rectilinear pieces in the Arts and Crafts tradition that found the most cordial reception. This acceptance was first reflected in the enthusiasm manifested during the 1870s and 1880s for furnishings in the Eastlake style (colorplate 15). It is true, of course, that the American version was often much embellished with gilding, ebony and carving (see plate 47 and colorplate 16), to an extent that proved intolerable to its author. But the fact remained that American Eastlake furniture was a considerable step beyond the exaggerated rococo and Renaissance revival pieces that had dominated North American parlors and dining rooms during previous decades. Moreover, in certain areas such as the use of stained glass, American manufacturers offered some attractive innovations (plate 50).

However, those Americans who sought after quality and simplicity in their furniture continued the quest for reform. Among their guides in this pilgrimage were Elbert Hubbard (1856–1915) and Gustav

Colorplate 17.
Design for a cabinet created by the American designer Will H. Bradley. Though far better known for his graphics, Bradley was also an advanced furniture designer. His pieces, which owe much to Mackintosh and the Glasgow School, proved too revolutionary for general acceptance in the United States. American, 1901–02. Private collection

Colorplate 18.
Fall-front desk, oak with brass fittings. The stark simplicity of this piece is typical of the functional designs favored by Gustav Stickley. American, c. 1901. Brooklyn Museum, H. Randolph Fund

Stickley (1857–1942), the two foremost exponents of the Arts and Crafts style in the United States. Hubbard, the heir to the Larkin pharmaceutical fortune, visited William Morris in England in 1894 and was so impressed with the design and quality of the books being turned out by Morris's Kelmscott Press in Hammersmith that he decided to open his own printing shop at East Aurora, not far from Buffalo, New York. There too Hubbard established the Roycroft Community, an association of artists and craftsmen based on the English Arts and Crafts guilds.

Founded in 1895, the community began in 1900 to manufacture furniture under the title of Roycroft Industries. The pieces were almost entirely handmade of native woods (oak was favored) and were extremely plain in design (plate 51). Chests, desks, dressers and even baby cribs were manufactured; not too surprisingly, it was an Americanized version of the Morris chair that proved most popular.

Each piece of Roycroft furniture was made by a single person and to order; that is, no stock was maintained. In keeping with the cooperative concept, copper upholstery tacks and hardware were made in the guild copper shop; even the leather upholstery was prepared on the premises. Furniture made in this way had to be expensive, and by 1910, competition from much cheaper mass-produced imitations had forced Hubbard to limit his line to a few items. The guild shops carried on even after Hubbard was drowned in the sinking of the *Lusitania* in 1915, but by 1938 the Depression had proved too much, and production ceased.

A sometime associate of Hubbard's was Will H. Bradley (1868–1962), a noted graphic designer who also turned his hand to furniture. Bradley's designs (colorplate 17) were strongly influenced by those of Charles Rennie Mackintosh's Glasgow School, whose work reflected both Art Nouveau and Arts and Crafts characteristics.

Stickley was more ambitious than Hubbard and more innovative—in part, no doubt, because he had been trained as a chairmaker. He too was greatly influenced by the English reformers. In 1898 he traveled to England to meet one of them, the British designer Charles F. A. Voysey, and his consequent new awareness of Arts and Crafts design caused him to greatly modify the style of the furniture he was making at his newly founded factory in Eastwood outside Syracuse, New York. From then on, Stickley's pieces had the rough-hewn, four-square look for which they are so well known (colorplate 18 and plate 52). Stickley made few bones about his dislike for the current revival styles, stating in a 1907 issue of his design magazine, *The Craftsman*, that a Stickley chair is "first, last and all the time a chair, and not an imitation of a throne, nor an exhibit of snakes and dragons in a wild riot of misapplied wood-carving. The fundamental purpose in building this chair was to make a piece which should be essentially comfortable, durable, well proportioned and as soundly put together as the best workmanship, tools and materials made possible."

51.
Magazine pedestal, quarter-sawn white oak. This piece was made by and bears the mark of Roycroft Industries of East Aurora, New York, an important manufacturer of American Arts and Crafts furnishings. American, c. 1908–12. Virginia Museum of Fine Arts, Richmond

52

53

52.
Library table, oak and leather with brass tacks and revealed construction. Designed by Gustav Stickley, a social reformer and creative innovator in furniture design, this piece reflects the American interpretation of the English Arts and Crafts style. American, 1906. Metropolitan Museum of Art, New York, gift of Cyril Farny in memory of Phyllis Holt, 1976

53.
High-back chair, oak, by Charles Rohlfs of Buffalo, New York. Though not as widely known as Gustav Stickley or Elbert Hubbard, Rohlfs was considerably more advanced in his design concepts. American, 1901. Cooper-Hewitt Museum, purchase by Mary Blackwelder Memorial Fund

Stickley's furniture was first exhibited at the 1900 furniture fair in Grand Rapids, Michigan, which was then the very home of cheap, mass-produced furnishings. While it would not be fair to say that his designs took the country by storm, they certainly contrasted sharply with the generally shoddy, overblown revival creations most other manufacturers offered. And they attracted customers.

Like Hubbard's, Stickley's pieces were sturdily made of oak, maple or other local timber; even mahogany was sometimes employed. In the earlier period the chief designer was Harvey Ellis, whose work is characterized by modest inlay decoration, heavy brass fittings, arched bases and a sparsity of line verging on the aesthetic. But Stickley himself also created pieces for the factory, and his even more austere examples came to dominate production.

Perhaps the most innovative of the American designers was Charles Rohlfs (1853–1936) of Buffalo, New York. Working at the turn of the century with fewer than a dozen assistants, Rohlfs produced a variety of pieces that combined Arts and Crafts construction and certain aspects of Art Nouveau decoration (plate 53). Rohlfs's output was never large, and his examples are much harder to come by than those of Stickley and Roycroft.

American Arts and Crafts furniture came to be known as Mission style, a misnomer since the Southwestern cottonwood and pine pieces once made in the Spanish missions were based on seventeenth-century Spanish prototypes and bore little real resemblance to the finely handcrafted pieces produced by Stickley and Hubbard that were, of course, based on English designs.

Nor were these the only manufacturers in the style. In 1900, two of Gustav's brothers formed the L. & J. G. Stickley Company to manufacture comparable pieces; and the Limbert and Lifetime lines were equally competitive and well made. In the end, it was not quality competition that put an end to Stickley's business. Rather, he himself, like Hubbard, succumbed to changing tastes and to an influx of cheap, mass-produced oak furniture in the Mission style. These furnishings mimicked the revealed construction and plain look of the real thing while really faking it with screws, nails, factory turnings and all the elements the originators had opposed. By 1916, Stickley was out of business.

5   Art Nouveau

The attitudes and activities that fed the English Arts and Crafts movement were generally accepted throughout Europe and North America. Yet the results in terms of design did not always find favor. In France, especially, designers who otherwise fully supported the reformers' concern for honest workmanship and distaste for cheap, factory-produced goods found it difficult to accept the severe, rectilinear quality of much Arts and Crafts furniture. They sought something softer, something more organic.

This appeared in the 1880s in the form of a new, almost ethereal style, whose dominant characteristic was the curve, and whose inspiration was a strange mixture of the romanticism that had fired the Arts and Crafts movement and the reliance on technology it so strongly opposed. From the former came a renewed interest in nature and a preference for organic forms that when literally interpreted might lead to the extreme of lamps with bases and stands imitating tree trunks. From the latter came the desire to experiment with new materials and at least a partial acceptance of the machine's role in production—a concession that foreshadowed the modern age just around the corner.

Some critics have argued that Art Nouveau was nothing more than the old rococo forms reborn with new, more organic decoration. But the varying development that the movement took in different countries, and its almost total failure in others (chiefly the United States), argues strongly that it was, in fact, a new and distinct style—one of the few to appear during the Victorian era.

Yet the new grows out of the old. Art Nouveau may be traced directly back to the reformers of the Arts and Crafts movement: a dependence reflected in an early French term for the mode, *le style Anglais*, which paid homage to the English pioneers of the new movement.

Colorplate 19.
Dressing table–sink, mahogany, ebony and marble with ceramic fixtures and gilt-bronze mounts. Designed by Louis Majorelle, one of the giants of the Nancy School, this piece of furniture exemplifies the naturalistic line favored by French Art Nouveau designers. French, 1900–1910. Metropolitan Museum of Art, New York, gift of Sydney and Frances Lewis Foundation, 1979

54.
Side chair, oak. The Scottish designer of this chair, Charles Rennie Mackintosh, is regarded as one of the most influential turn-of-the-century designers, though his English contemporaries dubbed him and his followers the "Spook School" because of their preference for elongated shapes and dead white color. Scottish, 1900. Museum of Modern Art, New York, gift of the Glasgow School of Art

For it was in England that men trained in the reformist philosophy began to strike out in a different direction. One of these was Arthur Heygate Mackmurdo (1851–1942). Though he had been associated with Morris and had been one of the founders of the Arts and Crafts movement, Mackmurdo in the early 1880s began to embellish his furnishings with sinuous, flamelike designs that seemed strangely out of place on their rectilinear surfaces. This combination of curvilinear, plantlike decoration and square or rectangular forms in rich, native woods proved popular to discerning critics, though their number was always small. The Art Nouveau was never able to surpass the Arts and Crafts mode in the British Isles.

One of the designers who moved against the tide was Mackmurdo's protégé, Charles Francis Annesley Voysey (1857–1941). Voysey had been a designer of wallpaper and textiles; his furniture, first seen at the Arts and Crafts Exhibition of 1893, revealed the work of a graphic designer who used the flat surfaces of traditional reformist pieces as a canvas on which to paint a new, curvilinear picture. In these decorative compositions, Voysey utilized organic forms such as the tulip and the thistle, as well as Oriental motifs reflecting his great interest in Japanese art, a source that was to prove important to most Art Nouveau designers.

However, Voysey was not content merely to decorate. Following the path blazed by Mackmurdo, he began to give English furniture a new vertical dimension. His chairs developed high backs, while sideboards and cupboards were supported by narrow legs and high columns terminating in the flat, square "mortarboard" caps that became characteristic of much Art Nouveau design. Voysey's pieces were still generally very much within the conservative Arts and Crafts tradition, yet they were never popular in England. They created a sensation on the Continent, however, where critics in France and Germany hailed their creator as a major figure in the new mode.

One of the most important and innovative British designers in the Art Nouveau tradition and one who gained great favor abroad was Charles Rennie Mackintosh (1868–1928). His furnishings were shown at the Vienna Sezession Exhibition of 1900, at the French Exposition Universelle held in Paris the same year, and at the Turin Exhibition of 1902. Mackintosh was trained and worked primarily in Glasgow, Scotland, and his physical distance from London may in part explain his divergence from the traditional Arts and Crafts approach. Certainly his work is more clearly related to the dominant Continental styles than that of any other British designer. Like Robert Adam, Mackintosh was an admirer of the total environment, so to some extent his furniture achieves its optimum effect in the homes for which it was designed. In any environment, though, it remains remarkable.

Mackintosh preferred tall, slender forms and small areas of rich, controlled decoration, incorporating inlay, paint and stained glass.

Some of his chairs were over six feet tall (plate 54) and in some cases were painted dead white—a distinction that led certain critics to refer to him and those designers who followed his lead as members of the "Spook School." Mackintosh's group, more properly known as the Glasgow School since its members had been educated and worked there, provided the most uniform and influential expression of the British Art Nouveau during the 1890s.

Other British exponents of the new mode were Mackay Hugh Baillie Scott (1865–1945), designer of the so-called Manx-style furniture, which in its verticality was related to the products of the Glasgow School, and George Walton (1867–1933), one of the very few self-taught furniture designers of the nineteenth century.

The innovations of individuals like Voysey and Mackintosh had great effect on Continental designers. Interestingly enough, these influences were to a substantial extent the result of commercial exportation of mass-produced pieces by manufacturers such as Liberty's of London. This firm, which was founded in 1875 to sell Oriental imports, was owned by Sir Arthur Lasenby Liberty (1843–1917), a friend of various Arts and Crafts designers. During the 1890s, Liberty's produced large numbers of well-built Art Nouveau pieces, many taken from Voysey designs. So great an influence did these exports have on taste in other areas of the Western world that in Italy, for example, Art Nouveau was known as *Stile Liberty*.

It was in Belgium, however, that the theories of Mackintosh and the Glasgow School really took hold, due in large part to the work of two architect-designers, Henry van de Velde (1863–1957) and Victor Horta (1861–1947). The first of these, van de Velde, proved to be one of the greatest theoreticians of the Art Nouveau movement. Trained originally as an artist, he was active in "Les Vingt," an important group of late nineteenth-century Belgian painters. Through this association he became aware of the ideas of William Morris and, eventually, of Charles Rennie Mackintosh's designs.

Like these men, van de Velde saw the house and its contents as a whole; the great bulk of his furnishings were created for specific rooms and specific situations. His earliest pieces (about 1893) were in a Gothic mode, but by 1896, when he was called to Paris to assist in the interior design and furnishing of Samuel Bing's shop, L'Art Nouveau (an interior that had an important influence on the French Art Nouveau movement), van de Velde had begun to work in the fluid patterns of the new mode (plate 55).

Line was of great importance to van de Velde, and his pieces were distinctly architectural—a characteristic of most Belgian Art Nouveau that allied it with the English style and set it off sharply from the more voluptuous French manner. Van de Velde also initially shared the English preference for native woods, but by 1900 he had abandoned oak and beech for mahogany and other exotic timbers, and had begun to paint his pieces white in the manner of Mackintosh. At this time his influence in the movement was at its height, due in no small part to the publication in 1901 of his major theoretical work, *Die Renaissance im modernen Kunstgewerbe*. His services as a consultant were sought throughout Europe. In 1901, he was appointed director of the Weimar Kunstgewerbeschule (Weimar School for Arts and Crafts) under the patronage of the Grand Duke of Saxe-Weimar-Gotha, and during the period preceding World War I he designed and furnished various German public buildings.

Equally important was the work of Victor Horta. More an architect than a furniture designer, Horta astounded Belgium with his very individualistic style, which featured highly modernistic open interiors and exposure of the building structure. Declaring that he had "abandoned the flower and leaf and turned instead to the stalk," Horta laid bare the beams, window frames and stairways of his houses, making the structural elements a part of the overall decorative pattern.

Not surprisingly, he treated furnishings in the same way. Chairs, tables and cupboards were viewed as inseparable from the rooms in which they stood, and were designed to fit within certain specific areas. This, of course, was also the philosophy of Mackintosh and

55.
Piano bench, pine lacquered in black, by Henry van de Velde. A prominent exponent of Art Nouveau, van de Velde had a profound effect on the development of the style in Europe. Belgian, c. 1907. Museum of Decorative Arts, Ghent

56.
Salon ensemble, oak. These pieces were designed by Victor Horta, whose highly abstract designs served as inspiration to various French Art Nouveau designers, including Hector Guimard. Belgian, c. 1894–95. Museum of Decorative Arts, Ghent

van de Velde, and like theirs, Horta's pieces often look a little odd when removed from their original context.

Horta totally abhorred the straight line. In an attempt to achieve fluidity in furniture design, he first modeled his new creations in clay, a technique employed too by the Frenchman Hector Guimard and one that would have been utterly repugnant to the "truth to materials" concept of the English reformers. Horta also loved exotic woods and lavish decoration, and would use anything for effect—including semi-precious stones, Oriental silks and even crocodile skins. In his somewhat outrageous experimentation he was more akin to the French designers than the English, though his approach was always more abstract and less naturalistic than that of his Gallic contemporaries (plate 56).

Two other important proponents of the notably three-dimensional and plastic Art Nouveau favored by the Belgian School were Gustave Serrurier-Bovy (1858–1910) and Paul Hankar (1859–1901). The latter, while greatly affected by English prototypes, was also an enthusiast of the art of the East, and his somewhat ponderous furnishings may reflect Oriental techniques in both construction and decoration. Serrurier-Bovy, too, was influenced by both the theory and the design of the Arts and Crafts movement, though his most characteristic design element—curved supports that create the impression of a series of arches—was distinctly Continental.

The work done in Belgium, England and particularly Germany was very important in formulating the new style. But it was in France that Art Nouveau reached its most expressive realization. Indeed, the phrase *Art Nouveau*, or New Art, originated in the title of the mercantile establishment opened in 1895 on the Rue de Provence in Paris by Samuel (Siegfried) Bing (1838–1905), a German-born impresario. Bing knew people working in the new styles who were in opposition to the socially entrenched revival modes, and he decided to sell the art and furnishings of this new age. As we have seen, Bing chose the Belgian van de Velde to assist in the designing of his shop, L'Art Nouveau; and Bing's art pavilion at the 1900 Exposition Universelle, which stunned Paris to such an extent that the term *le style 1900* became synonymous with the new mode, was designed in part by a Dutchman, Georges de Feure.

Nevertheless, the style that evolved in France was distinctly national, with an exaggerated emphasis on curvilinear patterns that owed an obvious debt to the baroque and rococo periods. The basic design vocabulary was based on an idealized abstraction of natural forms and featured most prominently a long S-shaped line terminating in a whiplike tendril. In some cases the preference for vegetative forms was so strong that furnishings would actually assume the shapes of recognizable trees, plants and flowers; but in most instances such specifics would be replaced with a flowing, undulating line.

Although the opening of Bing's shop lent a focus to the movement, and the 1900 Exposition is generally regarded as marking its zenith, Art Nouveau had begun to develop in France some years before. In the town of Nancy a group of craftsmen and designers had come together in the early 1880s to produce glass and other household accessories in what they perceived to be a "natural" style. This implied both a reverence for handwork and an admiration for decorative devices and forms derived from nature.

Foremost among these men was Émile Gallé (1846–1904), one of the world's great craftsmen in glass. Gallé began to design furniture in 1885, and his first examples, though clearly indebted to the rococo in form, already showed in their decoration the new predilection for organic motifs. A later example is seen in plate 57.

His training with glass oriented Gallé toward plasticity, however, and he quickly moved into the realm of sculptural fantasy. His pieces, which were given such exotic labels as "butterfly bed" and "dragon-fly table," assumed a powerful organic force and a form incorporating more or less realistic renditions of leaves, flowers, tree trunks and living creatures. The technical problems presented in rendering such designs in wood led to opposition from other designers of the day as well as from followers of the Arts and Crafts movement who saw the effort, in itself, as an affront to the basic relationship between a workman and his materials. But Gallé persisted in his designs and in defending his position in such important design publications as the *Revue des arts décoratifs.*

57.
Side chair, walnut inlaid with fruitwood, by Émile Gallé. Better known as a glass-maker, Gallé was an important force in all aspects of the development of French Art Nouveau and the leader of the branch of the movement located at Nancy. French, c. 1895. Cooper-Hewitt Museum, gift of Mrs. Jefferson Patterson

Colorplate 20.
Sofa and matching side chair, from a suite, hardwood carved and gilded, covered in silk needlepoint. Attributed to Louis Majorelle. French, c. 1910. Cooper-Hewitt Museum, gift of Mrs. Peter J. Perry

Under Gallé's direction, the Nancy School exerted a powerful influence on the direction of Art Nouveau design. In part this was due to the quality of the designers who came to be influenced by Émile Gallé's ideas, particularly Louis Majorelle (1859–1926). Trained as an artist in Paris, Majorelle returned to Nancy, his native town, in 1879. His family had run a furniture factory there, and he continued for some years to produce traditional pieces in the various revival styles, especially the rococo. Then in the early nineties he fell under the influence of Gallé, and by 1897 he was producing furniture in the Art Nouveau mode.

While he wholeheartedly supported his master's naturalistic theories, Majorelle, unlike almost all other furniture designers of the period, had been trained as a cabinetmaker. This seems to have created in him not only a great reverence for wood but also an innate conservatism, which made it impossible for him to accept some of the more extreme flights of fancy indulged in by Gallé and other designers.

His work as a result relies more on line than on decoration, and some pieces show an almost classical restraint in which the only clearly new art feature is the basic outline. Majorelle himself stated clearly that, "whatever the function of a piece of furniture, the craftsman must ensure that the lines can exist without decoration. . . . The richness of a piece of furniture should owe nothing to a surfeit of decoration. . . ." In keeping with this philosophy, he preferred richly grained woods such as mahogany and walnut, and often used marquetry or inlay in contrasting darks and lights. Moreover, he employed gilding and gilt bronze far more frequently than most of his peers.

Though perhaps not the most creative designer of the era, Majorelle was clearly one of the more successful. While he could achieve a rich, naturalistic form in his pieces (colorplate 19), Majorelle tended for the most part to create suites of elegant and refined furnishings recognizably Art Nouveau in form but sufficiently conservative in decoration to satisfy a wide traditionalist audience (colorplate 20). His factory at Nancy consequently became the nation's largest and most prosperous producer of furniture in the new mode.

Another group of Art Nouveau designers was based in Paris. Centered upon the Bing emporium, this loose coalition of designers was open to foreign influence—chiefly from England, Belgium and Germany. More abstract and stylized than the Nancy examples, Art Nouveau pieces from Paris also owed less to prior styles such as the rococo. The major figures in the Parisian School were Edward Colonna (1862–1948), Georges de Feure (1868–1928) and Eugène Gaillard (1862–1933). It was these three men who designed Bing's new art pavilion for the 1900 Exposition Universelle, and they had substantial influence on those who were drawn to the movement through what they saw at this exposition.

De Feure, a Dutchman, was one of the few in that nation who were drawn to the Art Nouveau mode. Trained as both artist and designer,

58.
Display cabinet, carved wood and glass. This cabinet was designed by Edward Colonna, and illustrates his preference for tall, narrow furnishings with minimal decoration. French, c. 1900–1902. Museum für Kunst und Gewerbe, Hamburg

59.
Cabinet, carved wood, glass and gilt bronze. The convoluted, plastic form marks this piece as one by Hector Guimard, a Parisian contemporary of Victor Horta. French, c. 1902–5. Musée des Arts Décoratifs, Paris

58

59

he produced fine glassware and some important posters, as well as furniture of a highly sculptural quality.

De Feure was closer to Bing, but Edward Colonna was probably the most important designer in the group. Extremely versatile, he worked in such diverse mediums as ceramics, metal, textiles and of course wood. At the exposition he created roomsful of stark, attenuated furniture set against a background of green velvet. As far as the new art was concerned, he could best be described as a minimalist, for his furnishings were tall and spare of line, with a minimum of decoration and a delicacy that made them appear to float above the floor (plate 58).

The pieces produced by Eugène Gaillard were more massive and more dynamic, with a resemblance in line to those of Majorelle. As an interior designer, his specialty was the dining area and the bedroom, and he created a variety of pieces for these spaces.

Paris was an important center of the new mode, but not all of its practitioners chose to work with Bing. One of the mavericks was Hector Guimard (1867–1942), an architect and designer who studied at the École des Arts Décoratifs. Guimard had been influenced in his formative period by the abstracted natural forms favored by his contemporary Horta, and he too created writhing, curvilinear forms so contorted it often seemed impossible they could have been made from wood. Not surprisingly, he also preferred to model a piece in clay and then turn the result over to his assistants for transformation into wood—a task that did not always prove possible.

His debt to Horta aside, Guimard worked essentially alone. He had little to do with other designers of the era, and his work was highly individualistic. These factors led to his being misunderstood, particularly by critics who objected to his exaggerated form and decoration while failing to see that his abbreviation and amplification of natural forms was the inevitable result of the design premises behind the new mode. Guimard's work also suffered from the fact that, like Horta, he designed for a specific space and purpose. His pieces were created to fit in a particular spot, and out of context they may appear somewhat strange (plate 59).

Guimard nonetheless attained considerable prominence in the movement. He designed numerous interiors, and during the period 1899–1904 created the extraordinary cast-iron entrances whose facades of writhing plant life, fish and insects for so long framed the approaches to the Paris Métro stations. Though he worked in metal and in clay as well, Guimard always preferred wood. His earliest pieces (pre-1900) are in mahogany, but in his period of greatest activity, the first decade of the twentieth century, he employed pear, which was easier to bend and steam into the convoluted shapes he required (plate 60).

Two other important designers active in Paris were Alexandre Charpentier (1856–1909) and Alphonse Mucha (1860–1939). Charpentier was a sculptor and a member of the Parisian group known as "Les Six." His early furnishings were rectilinear in the Arts and Crafts manner, but in the first years of the present century he embraced the new art. Many of his pieces feature heavily carved sculptural figures. Though far better known as one of the era's greatest poster designers, Mucha also created some furniture. His work tends to be lightly decorated and extremely fluid, possessing a simple dynamism that foreshadows the furniture of the Modern movement (plate 61).

Art Nouveau reached its point of fullest acceptance with the 1900 Exposition Universelle in Paris. By 1905 the movement had run out of creative steam and was becoming progressively more stereotyped, particularly in France, where by 1910 new design ideas were taking hold. In other areas of Europe the style never attained comparable popularity. Spain had but a single disciple, though he was a giant: the extraordinary architect and designer Antonio Gaudí y Cornet (1852–1926). Trained as a coppersmith, Gaudí showed the same interest in plasticity of form evinced by Horta and Guimard. In architecture he had no peer during the period, while his bizarre furniture, which featured iron spider- or stalklike legs and surfaces almost swallowed up by the organic forms supporting them, attracted more attention than buyers. Indeed, Gaudí was quite alone in Spain in his interest in the Art Nouveau, for his generally conservative peers spent the era recycling the furnishings of past dynasties.

60.
Frame, fruitwood, partly gilt, designed by Hector Guimard. French, 1905–10. Cooper-Hewitt Museum, gift of Madame Hector Guimard

61

Colorplate 21.
Secretary in walnut with decoration and inlay in vellum, copper and pewter. The work of Carlo Bugatti, creator of this unique example, spans the era between the Victorian and the Modern periods. Italian, c. 1888–1902. Metropolitan Museum of Art, New York, Edward C. Moore, Jr., Gift Fund, 1969

61.
Low table, carved wood and leather. Designed by Alphonse Mucha, this small piece in its simplicity of line and use of natural materials foreshadows many directions in twentieth-century furnishings. French, c. 1900. Musée des Arts Décoratifs, Paris

62.
Chair, walnut, brass, pewter and vellum. Designed by Carlo Bugatti to match the secretary seen in colorplate 21, this piece shows a definite Oriental inspiration. Italian, c. 1888–1902. Metropolitan Museum of Art, New York, Rogers Fund, 1970

The new art found more adherents in Italy, where its development was influenced by both English and French interpretations. Initially the winds blew from the British Isles, and Italy's most prominent interpreters of the mode, Carlo Bugatti (1855–1940) and Eugenio Quarti (1867–1931), were exponents of the rectilinear English designs dubbed *Stile Liberty*.

Bugatti is by far the more remarkable of the two, and while his furnishings are generally regarded as falling within the scope of Arts and Crafts–Art Nouveau, they are so highly individualistic as to defy easy placement. Their general rectilinear outlines reflect Bugatti's awareness of the English reformers, but their wholesale incorporation of pseudo-Moorish, Greek and Egyptian motifs is more reminiscent of late nineteenth-century revival styles (colorplate 21 and plate 62).

Eugenio Quarti's work is considerably more traditional, even though he was an apprentice in Bugatti's shop in Milan from 1888 until late in the century. When he did begin to work independently around 1900, he produced symmetrical, well-balanced pieces with great clarity of form (plate 63). Carving and decoration were kept to a minimum, and simplicity and refinement were emphasized.

The French influence is much more evident in the work of Carlo Zen, who was active as a designer in the period 1898–1902. The flowing outlines of Zen furnishings were bold enough to satisfy anyone in the Parisian School, though he set himself apart through an emphasis on remarkably delicate inlay that is distinctly Japanese in quality. It

62

is known that Carlo Zen was much affected by his observation of Japanese calligraphy and lacquerware, and his delicate wood, metal and mother-of-pearl inlay is strongly Oriental in concept if not in execution (plate 64).

Though relatively few Italian designers worked in the *Stile Liberty*, their writings and creations had an important effect on the nation's attitude toward design and served to pave the way for the introduction of modern concepts as these were explored and developed in Germany and France. The effects of the new art were felt in Austria as well as in Germany, and the form these effects eventually took there foreshadowed an end to Art Nouveau and the development of what has come to be regarded as typical twentieth-century design.

In Germany, the philosophy of Morris and the techniques of Mackintosh were merged in the *Jugendstil*, a form of linear Art Nouveau that took its name from *Jugend*, a weekly on the arts that first appeared in 1896. Also known as *Neue Stil*, the German mode found most of its supporters in Munich and Darmstadt. Its new design concepts were brought to public attention initially through the Seventh International Arts Exhibition, held at Dresden in 1897.

63.
Vitrine table, mahogany and glass with inlay in various woods. Designed by Eugenio Quarti. Italian, c. 1901–2. Cooper-Hewitt Museum, gift of Signora Marie-Louise Wanner Quarti

64.
Writing desk and chair, fruitwood inlaid with brass, white metal and mother-of-pearl. Designed by Carlo Zen, who was active in Milan at the turn of the century, these furnishings reflect a high degree of sophistication and considerable knowledge of Oriental decorative techniques. Italian, 1902. Cooper-Hewitt Museum: gifts of John Goodwin (desk) and Donald Vlack (chair)

63

64

From the very beginning Jugendstil design was extremely eclectic, reflecting the preferences of individual artists for such diverse sources as the medieval, the Oriental and the Renaissance, as well as traditional German folk forms. As an example, one of its leading figures, August Endell (1871–1925), combined Japanese and Near Eastern decorative motifs with voluptuous and fantastic forms reminiscent of Horta and Gaudí at their wildest. Another member of the Munich group, Richard Riemerschmid (1868–1957), supported the "organic" theory of furniture design and construction, and preferred functional forms with only the most limited decoration and an emphasis on wood grain.

The tendency of Arts and Crafts devotees to band together in groups was not lost on the Germans, and among the more important of such homegrown associations were the united workshops, or *Vereinigte Werkstätten*, which were established in Munich in 1898. Intended to bring together artisans and designers working in the Jugendstil, these organizations were much influenced by the theories and work of Riemerschmid and Endell. When they were replaced in 1907 by the newly created German Craft Union, or *Deutscher Werkbund*, this largely signaled the end of German Art Nouveau and its replacement by a newer, more machine-oriented approach.

Darmstadt, the other German center of the Jugendstil, owed its existence to the benevolence of the Grand Duke of Hesse-Darmstadt who, in 1899, invited a group of German and Austrian scholars to live and work at the artists' colony of Mathildehöhe. The leading figure in this association was Peter Behrens (1868–1940). As at Munich, an initial predilection among the membership for the dreamy and organic in the Art Nouveau gradually was replaced by an angular and more functional style.

In Austria, resistance to the new design concepts was encountered from those who favored the prevailing eclectic revival styles, and the birth of the movement was a dramatic one. A group of young artists and designers, annoyed at the choice by the Vienna Municipal Council in 1897 of an exhibition pavilion design submitted by two traditionalist architects, resigned from the local visual arts society and founded the Association of Austrian Visual Artists. Their departure from the paths of tradition came to be called the *Sezession*, a name applied in due course to the Austrian version of Art Nouveau.

The Sezession was almost immediately successful, not only in Vienna (which remained its greatest center of influence) but in other Austrian cities as well. By 1898 the group already had a building of its own design, regular annual exhibitions of its members' work and a publication, *Ver Sacrum*. Leading figures in the movement were Josef Hoffmann (1870–1956) and Joseph Maria Olbrich (1867–1908).

65.
Bentwood side chair, beech and leather. Manufactured by Thonet Brothers, this piece was designed by Josef Hoffmann, a leading exponent of the Sezession, the Austrian version of Art Nouveau. Austrian, 1903–6. Cooper-Hewitt Museum, combined funds and Crane & Co.

Hoffmann, in particular, cast a long shadow. He was a brilliant teacher as well as a designer and architect, and his ideas influenced several generations of European designers. He too had initially preferred the curve, as reflected in the bentwood furniture of Thonet, for whom he had designed (plate 65). But his interest proved to be more in construction than in decoration, a factor that inevitably led him away from the surface-oriented aspects of Art Nouveau toward square or rectangular forms and the interrelationships of flat surfaces.

In 1903 Hoffmann established with Kolo Moser (1868–1918) the *Wiener Werkstätte*, a cooperative venture largely founded on Arts and Crafts principles. The Werkstätte sought to bring designers and craftsmen closer together and to provide a place where complete interiors from wallpaper to furniture could be created as part of a single design. Though its personnel and theory changed over the years, the Werkstätte survived into the early 1930s, and it played a major role in the development of both German and Austrian design.

Olbrich, who had created the Sezession exhibition building in Vienna, was an equally versatile designer of metalwork, of jewelry and of furniture. His presence at Mathildehöhe in the early 1900s served to unify to some extent the Austrian and German versions of Art Nouveau. Other leading lights in the Sezession were Otto Wagner (1841–1918), who had taught both Hoffmann and Olbrich, and whose credo, "Nothing that is not practical can be beautiful," became manifest in their work, and Gustav Klimt (1862–1918), a painter and designer who was first president of the new group and who had vast influence on German interior decoration during the early years of this century.

The German and Austrian versions of Art Nouveau were, almost from the beginning, substantially different from the French version. In this divergence they were in basic agreement with the English and the Belgians, who also came to favor simple, rectilinear forms and minimal decoration as opposed to the rich, flowing surfaces preferred by most French designers.

The Art Nouveau mode was widely followed in other areas of Europe as well, but oddly enough had little effect on American furniture design until the early twentieth century. Even then the furniture was for the most part inferior in quality, although the Tiffany Glass and Decorating Company, which produced excellent glass and metal accessories, also turned out some credible furniture (plate 66). By 1910, except in France and Italy, the geometric had won out, heralding a new age—one in which function would be the basic design criterion and the machine the basic producer.

66.
Armchair, maple inlaid with various metals. Art Nouveau furnishings did not appear in the United States until around 1900. This piece is by the Tiffany Glass and Decorating Company of New York. American, c. 1900. Metropolitan Museum of Art, New York, gift of Mr. and Mrs. Georges Seligmann, 1964

6　The Modern Movement

By the end of the nineteenth century two distinct trends were evident in furniture design. On the one hand were the large commercial furniture manufacturers, such as those located in London and in the Grand Rapids area of the United States, employing machines to produce standardized, generally uninspired period furnishings for a mass market. On the other hand were the individuals and small groups of designers experimenting with different approaches to both design and manufacture.

In England the guildsmen of the Arts and Crafts movement were concerned with honesty in workmanship and materials, and gave priority to handwork, a decision that made it difficult for their products to reach a mass audience. On the Continent other designers—chiefly in Belgium, France and Germany—were attempting to fuse a more or less classical movement, the Art Nouveau, with the realities of an assembly-line world.

Eventually, the amalgamation that prevailed was one of form in the English manner (geometric and unadorned) and technique in the European manner, accepting the machine's dictates in furniture design. Of this union was born the Modern, or International, style, a method of furniture manufacture that knows no national boundaries or ethnic characteristics, and is essentially one of functional design for machine production and contemporary living.

The origins of the Modern style were many and varied. Certainly, Thonet's development of mass-produced, wooden-dowel furnishings was important, as was Belter's use of laminated wood and Morris's concern for revealed construction. But the movement did not owe its origin to any one man or group of men or to any particular advance in technique.

Colorplate 22.
Armchair, painted plywood, by Gerrit T. Rietveld. Closely associated with the artists of the De Stijl movement, Rietveld translated the geometric forms that absorbed the group into practical and functional furniture. Dutch, 1917. Museum of Modern Art, New York, gift of Philip Johnson

There is no doubt that much of the early creative work took place in Germany and Austria. The rectilinear style of the Glasgow School had far greater impact in these countries than it did in France. When Henry van de Velde was appointed director of the Weimar School for Arts and Crafts in 1901, he brought to the position not only his distinctive design concepts as a disciple of Morris and Mackintosh but also a firm belief in the role of the machine in production and a commitment to the unity of house and furnishings. It is on this foundation that the Modern movement stands.

It was not long before the effect of the new thought was being felt throughout central Europe. Jugendstil designers such as Richard Riemerschmid (who had designed a chair for machine production in 1899) and Josef Hoffmann began to create strongly rectilinear forms with a minimum of surface decoration; and the establishment in 1907 of the Deutscher Werkbund signaled a new direction, in that to the usual group of artisans, architects and interior designers there was added a coterie of manufacturers. All now worked with a common goal: to raise the standards of industrial design.

Among those active in the Werkbund was Walter Gropius (1883–1969), an architect and interior designer who was to prove a seminal figure in the movement. In 1914 Gropius succeeded van de Velde as director of the Weimar School, and five years later he reorganized the institution as *Das Staatliche Bauhaus* with the specific goal of training designers to create items for machine production. By 1925 Gropius had removed the Bauhaus to Dessau, where buildings of his own design were completed in 1926.

Before it was closed by the Nazi government in 1933, the Bauhaus had become the focal point of the Modern movement in furniture design. Its basic tenet—functionalism or creation for use—was not unique, having earlier been espoused by both the Arts and Crafts reformers and such designers as Otto Wagner. What was unique was the quality of designers drawn to the group and their ability to propagate their doctrine.

However, the Bauhaus designers themselves were substantially affected by outside sources, in particular the Dutch art movement known as *De Stijl* and its foremost design exponent, Gerrit T. Rietveld (1888–1964). The members of De Stijl advocated neoplasticism, and confined their compositions to asymmetrically arranged squares and circles. Rietveld adapted these in his revolutionary Red-Blue, or Berlin, chair of 1917 (colorplate 22), which was composed of two slabs of painted plywood screwed into a boxlike framework of squared timbers. The pure geometry of this piece owes much to cubist art, and it served as the prototype for many later seating items.

One of the Bauhaus designers most moved by De Stijl concepts was Marcel Breuer (b. 1902), a Hungarian by birth who came to the institute in 1920 and took charge of its carpentry shop in 1924. Breuer had designed several cubist-inspired wooden forms when, in 1925, he undertook creation of a tubular-steel chair. He was not the first in the field. In 1844 a Frenchman named Gandillot had welded some steel tubes together to create a chair, and Breuer's own immediate inspiration derived from looking at a set of bicycle handlebars. In totality of design, however, the chair was a major breakthrough, laying the groundwork for all modern steel furniture (plate 67).

Breuer's intention was to produce inexpensive, comfortable and good-looking pieces of seating furniture that could be readily mass-produced (colorplate 23). He chose chrome-plated tubular steel as his medium, noting that "mass production and standardization had already made me interested in polished metal, in shining and impeccable lines in space as new components for our interiors. I considered such polished and curved lines as not only symbolic of our modern technology but actually to be technology." Lighter and more fluid than the Rietveld chair, Breuer's creation bore some resemblance to mid-nineteenth-century Thonet furniture; and not surprisingly, the old Vienna firm adapted several of his Bauhaus designs from the 1925–28 period for commercial production.

Though attacked by some critics as cold, lacking in style and even "primitive," tubular steel quickly became one of the favorite mediums of the new-wave designers. Lightweight but strong, readily produced and shaped by machines, it held appeal for many. One of these was Ludwig Mies van der Rohe (1886–1969), an architect and designer of international status. Born in Aachen, Mies succeeded Gropius in 1930 as director of the Bauhaus and stayed until the school was shut down in 1933.

Prior to that time he had been first vice-president of the Deutscher Werkbund Exhibition of 1927 at Stuttgart, where International style furnishings were first exhibited en masse. The shock produced by this display was exceeded in 1929, when Mies presented his so-called Barcelona furniture at the Barcelona International Exhibition. Designed on the cantilever principle, these chairs and couches were framed in steel and cushioned with leather hung on strapping. Light but amazingly sturdy, they seemed almost to hover above the ground. During the next decade Mies continued to design a line of sophisticated metal-frame furniture (plate 68).

As innovative and practical as they seemed then and still do, these furnishings did not meet with universal acceptance and, indeed, had attracted little attention on the Continent before the Stuttgart Exhibition. Much of Europe was still making furniture in a more or less traditional manner. In England the Arts and Crafts mode remained generally in control, the major innovation being the introduction after World War I of quality factory-made furniture in this style. The man who took this step was Sir Ambrose Heal (1872–1959), the scion of a highly successful family of furniture makers. Heal recog-

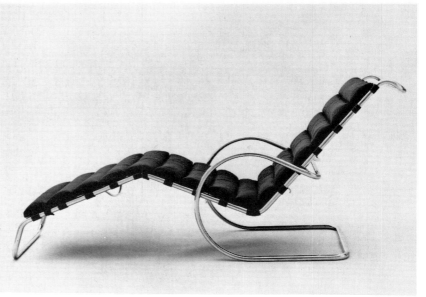

67.
Armchair, tubular steel and canvas. Designed by Marcel Breuer, this chair became the prototype for twentieth-century tubular-metal furnishings. German, 1925. Cooper-Hewitt Museum, gift of Gary Laredo

68.
Chaise longue, contour cushion on tubular-steel frame. Cantilever suspension, as promoted by Ludwig Mies van der Rohe, who created this piece, added a new dimension to furniture construction. German, 1932. Museum of Modern Art, New York, gift of Knoll International

69.
Transat chair, black lacquer frame, upholstered in padded leather. Eileen Gray, who designed this chair, was one of the few women designers of the early twentieth century. English, 1927. Private collection

68

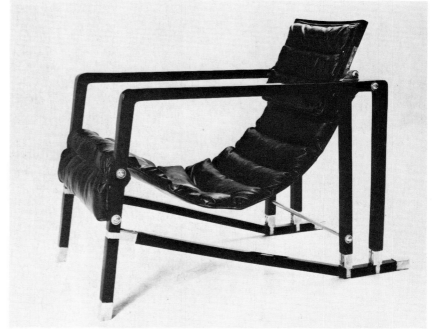

Colorplate 23.
Cesca armchair, chrome-plated tubular steel, celluloid and cane; designed by Marcel Breuer. German, 1928. Brooklyn Museum, New York, gift of Stendig Inc.

69

nized that English furniture could not compete in world markets without resort to factory methods, but he was also unwilling to give up the high standards set by the Arts and Crafts reformers. The result was a reasonable compromise: plain but attractive and well-built furnishings, which became known as "cottage furniture" and attained great popularity.

Heal's furnishings showed the traditional English preference for wood as material; ironically, the nation's most important designer in the Modern mode had to leave the country to gain recognition for her metal and lacquer pieces. This innovator, Eileen Gray (1879–1976), one of the earliest women designers to gain recognition, was originally an artist and an acknowledged master of lacquerwork. Then in the early 1920s, in Paris, she came under the influence of the Modern movement; thereafter, her pieces featured metal tubing, celluloid, glass and other materials heretofore regarded as "industrial" in nature. Though she was indirectly affected by the work of such men as Gropius and Mies van der Rohe, Gray was always her own person. Pieces like her Transat chair of 1927 (plate 69) reflect an innovative combination of industrial materials with the lacquer for which she was always noted.

Gray's ideas were not always well received even in France. The showing of her first interior (in 1923) was greeted with what she later described as "a torrent of abuse." In part this may have reflected the typical Gallic hostility to a woman who was challenging what had up to then been regarded as a man's world, but it certainly also reflected the fact that the "modern" at that time was very different in France from the work transpiring in Germany and Austria.

It was in France that designers had carried the organic line of Art Nouveau to its voluptuous extreme, and it was there also that the style had found its deepest traditional roots—in eighteenth-century rococo.

70.
Dining table, walnut. Designed by Lucien Lévy-Dhurmier, this piece reflects the lingering Art Nouveau tradition that dominated French furniture well into the present century. French, 1910–14. Metropolitan Museum of Art, New York, Harris Brisbane Dick Fund, 1966

So well founded a mode does not expire easily, and long after 1900 French designers like Lucien Lévy-Dhurmier (1865–1953) were still working in it (plate 70). However, as the new century progressed, the line became heavier and the carving more grotesque. The public—or rather, the tastemakers—yearned for something else. It appeared in 1909 with the arrival of Sergei Diaghilev's Ballet Russe. The staging and decor of the Russian ballet, with its emphasis on strong, clashing colors derived from ikon painting and Oriental traditions, took Paris by storm. Within weeks, designers of everything from clothing to jewelry were capitalizing on the new Eastern motifs.

In furniture design the reaction was less extreme. Rugs and pillows and rich textiles abounded, but the traditional element in French furnishings easily weathered the storm from the East. True, sofas and beds became lower in the Oriental manner and chairs grew higher backs and lower legs. But the basic forms of these pieces remained clearly recognizable, not as innovations but as reruns of eighteenth- and early nineteenth-century styles. What did change were the materials.

The French furniture materials now became more luxurious than anything known for a hundred years. Oak and walnut were replaced by such expensive imports as mahogany, amboyna, palisander and ebony. Marquetry, particularly inlay of mother-of-pearl, reappeared; and shagreen, a treated sharkskin or leather, became so popular as to be regarded as basic to the new style. Distinctly notable by their absence were the materials of industry—steel, aluminum, Bakelite, canvas and all the other humble ingredients of the Modern style.

This was no accident, for the French movement, which has recently come to be known as Art Deco (from its culmination in the Paris Exposition des Arts Décoratifs of 1925), was not truly modern, though in time it appropriated such features of the Modern movement as cubist decorative elements. On the contrary, Art Deco was firmly anchored in the past.

The truth of this is readily seen in the work of the epoch's greatest designer, Jacques-Émile Ruhlmann (1879–1933). Ruhlmann, who first showed his work at the Salon des Artistes Décorateurs in 1913, was a master of detail and an unabashed advocate of luxury. His shop specialized in finely veneered pieces, often inlaid with ivory, and the quality of workmanship was so high that he was commonly referred to as "the Riesener of the twentieth century" (see *Furniture 1*). It need hardly be added that furniture such as Ruhlmann's was both hand-made and extremely expensive, as was the norm for Art Deco throughout its most creative period. It was intended neither for the masses nor for mass production. Only after the full force of the Modern movement had been brought to bear on French culture in the early 1930s would designers begin to wrestle with the problems of adapting Art Deco fashions to factory manufacture.

71

71.
Lady's desk, Macassar ebony and ivory, designed by Jacques-Émile Ruhlmann. French, c. 1915–20. Metropolitan Museum of Art, New York, Edward C. Moore, Jr., Gift Fund, 1923

72.
Cabinet, palisander wood, veneered on mahogany with marble top; designed by Léon Jallot. French, c. 1920–30. Metropolitan Museum of Art, New York, Edward C. Moore, Jr., Gift Fund, 1925

Colorplate 24.
Desk, chair and file cabinet, amboyna wood, sharkskin, ivory and silvered bronze mounts. The creator of these sleek and luxurious pieces was Jacques-Émile Ruhlmann, the leading designer of the early twentieth century. French, c. 1918–28. Metropolitan Museum of Art, New York

Ruhlmann's furniture was always understated, relying for its impact on a general harmony and balance of line rather than any great amount of decoration, and its general configuration owed much to the Neoclassic (colorplate 24 and plate 71). His lead in this respect was followed by other designers of the epoch such as Léon Jallot (plate 72), Louis Süe (1875–1968), André Mare (1885–1932) and Jules-Émile Leleu (1883–1961). Süe and Mare were particularly active in the 1920s following their establishment in 1919 of a private design and decorating firm, Compagnie des Arts Français. Their pleasing but not very innovative designs (plates 73 and 74) were found in shops and in private homes, and graced the salons of the great ocean liners such as the *Normandie* and the *Île de France*. Leleu was another highly successful traditionalist (plate 75) whose decorating company survived into the present era. The work of these men and particularly that of Ruhlmann dominated the great Paris Exposition of 1925 and largely set the standards for what was then termed *Art Moderne* (the appellation *Art Deco* first being coined by revivalists in the 1960s).

73.
Desk and chair, ebony, gilt bronze and pigskin. Designed by Louis Süe and André Mare, these pieces reflect the massiveness that came to prevail in late, factory-made Art Deco. French, c. 1925. Metropolitan Museum of Art, New York, Edward C. Moore, Jr., Gift Fund, 1925

74

74.
Mirror, green and gold lacquer, designed by Louis Süe and André Mare. French, c. 1925–30. Metropolitan Museum of Art, New York, Edward C. Moore, Jr., Gift Fund, 1923

75.
Commode, amboyna wood and ivory with marble top. The traditional form of this piece by Jules-Émile Leleu reflects the classical heritage of the Art Deco style. French, c. 1925. Metropolitan Museum of Art, New York, gift of Agnes Miles Carpenter, 1946

75

However, there were some free spirits as well. Edgar Brandt did some interesting work in metal (plate 76), while Pierre Legrain (1889–1929) created elegant pieces in chrome and pale wood, and powerful stools, chairs and tables patterned on the African art that was then making such an impact on the Parisian art scene (plate 78). Other talents included Clément Rousseau (plate 77) and Jean-Michel Frank (colorplate 25), both of whom worked in such exotic materials as ebony, sharkskin and ivory, and Jean Dunand (1877–1942), who combined forms unusually rectilinear for the time and place (plate 79 and colorplate 1, see page 6) with a remarkable artistry in lacquer (plate 80) and a propensity for heroic shapes. Another skilled lacquerworker was Gaston Priou (colorplate 26).

The rich and sophisticated styling of the Art Deco seemed, by the mid-1920s, to have France firmly in its grasp. Designers were establishing their own decorating companies or contracting to have their work produced and sold through major department stores such as Bon Marché and Galéries Lafayette. Moreover, interest in the Gallic mode seemed to be spreading even into Germany, where Bruno Paul (1874–1968), an early exponent of the rectilinear and the first European to design unit furniture, was creating boudoir pieces with which few Art Deco exponents could have found fault (colorplate 27).

There was one small fly in the ointment. The great Paris Exposition of 1925 that was the crowning glory of the Deco movement was marred by the appearance of one Charles-Édouard Jeanneret-Gris, better known to posterity as Le Corbusier (1887–1965). A Swiss by birth, Le Corbusier was an architect and designer by profession and, by choice, an exponent of the Modern movement. Political differences had kept his German and Austrian colleagues at home, but he had come to Paris to lay claim to the future.

The officials of the exposition were not pleased to see him. Everything about his proposed exhibition pavilion, which he boldly and prophetically entitled "L'Esprit Nouveau," offended them: the structure itself, a stark example of his "system building," and most of all the contents—furnishings of plain steel and chrome with lines like machines and not a trace of lacquer, ebony, ivory or rare wood (plate 81 and colorplate 28).

Frustrated in their attempts to exclude him, the Parisian functionaries consigned Le Corbusier's exhibit to the most remote location they could find. Then, in case anyone managed to locate it, they surrounded the whole thing with an eighteen-foot wall. But, of course, one cannot wall up ideas; and despite the best efforts of the exponents of Art Deco, modernism came to France. In 1930, Le Corbusier, Eileen Gray and several other architects and designers founded the Union des Artistes Modernes, and the younger and bolder of France's designers began to flock to a new banner.

76.
Armchair, enameled wood, parchment and synthetic fibers, c. 1935, by Hammond Kroll (American, b. 1898), shown with French glass and metal mirror and bronze *torchère* with alabaster reflector, both c. 1925, by Edgar Brandt. Cooper-Hewitt Museum, gift of Mrs. Helen Kroll Kramer, in memory of Dr. Milton Lurie Kramer (armchair) and from the collection of the late Stanley Siegel, gift of Stanley Siegel (mirror and *torchère*)

77.
Table, ebony, sharkskin and ivory. Light and delicate as it may appear, the sharkskin surface of this table by Clément Rousseau made it almost impervious to stain or damage. French, 1922–29. Metropolitan Museum of Art, New York, Fletcher Fund, 1972

77

Colorplate 25.
Desk, covered in sharkskin, with ivory
drawer pulls, designed by Jean-Michel Frank.
French, c. 1935. Cooper-Hewitt Museum,
gift of Mr. and Mrs. Forsythe Sherfesee

Colorplate 26.
Three-paneled screen in wood and lacquer, attributed to Gaston Priou. Large screens such as this were popular salon decorations in the 1930s. They often depicted African or South Seas vistas. French, c. 1930. Brooklyn Museum, New York, Frank L. Babbott Fund

78

78.
Stool, rosewood carved in the African style, designed by Pierre Legrain. French, 1924. Metropolitan Museum of Art, New York, Fletcher Fund, 1972

79.
Table, lacquered wood with a top surfaced in crushed eggshell, designed by Jean Dunand. French, c. 1930. Cooper-Hewitt Museum, gift of Rodman A. Heeren

Colorplate 27.
Dressing table and stool, tulipwood and ivory with gilt-bronze fittings. Though created by one of the earliest members of the Modern movement, Bruno Paul, these pieces are distinctly Art Deco in feeling. German, c. 1924. Metropolitan Museum of Art, New York, gift of Ralph and Lester Weindling, 1976, in memory of Daly Weindling

79

Colorplate 28.
Cube chair, chrome and brown leather, designed by Le Corbusier, Pierre Jeanneret
and Charlotte Perriand. French, c. 1927.
Brooklyn Museum, New York, gift of Atelier International

80.
Three-panel screen entitled *Pianissimo*, lacquer and wood, designed by the master lacquerworker Jean Dunand. French, 1925–26. Metropolitan Museum of Art, New York, gift of Mrs. Solomon R. Guggenheim, 1950

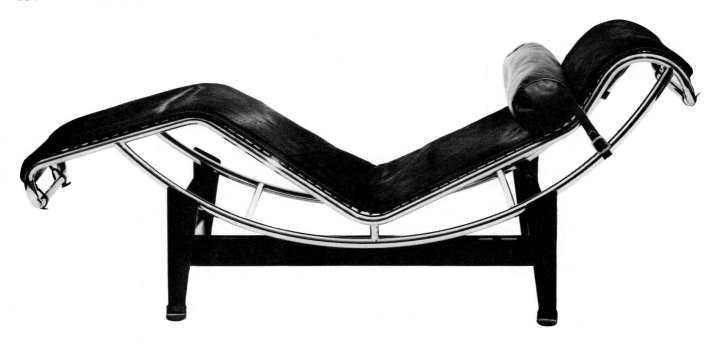

81.
Chaise longue, tubular and cast steel, leather contour padding, designed by the architect Le Corbusier and Charlotte Perriand, one of his collaborators in furniture design. Le Corbusier played a major role in introducing the International style to France. French, 1927. Brooklyn Museum, New York, gift of Atelier International

82.
Table, hardwood painted black. The designer of this table, Jules Bouy, like so many designers in North America at the time, was a European by birth. American, c. 1930–35. Metropolitan Museum of Art, New York, gift of Juliette B. Castle and Mrs. Paul Dahlstrom, 1968

83.
Desk, tulipwood and ebony veneer with metal mounts, designed by Jules Bouy and typical of the forms that were mass-produced in the United States from 1925 until World War II. American, c. 1930–35. Metropolitan Museum of Art, New York, gift of Juliette B. Castle and Mrs. Paul Dahlstrom, 1968

Art Deco did not just go away. It continued, with diminishing vitality, through the 1930s. There were some changes. The dominance of geometry had its effect in a gradual replacement of curvilinear forms with square or rectangular ones, and as the Depression deepened, designers turned more and more to public rather than private commissions. Ocean liners and public buildings throughout France were decorated in the Deco mode. Such work was usually on a large scale, and a resultant coarsening of the style took place, heightened by the adaptation of certain pieces to mass production. Nevertheless Art Deco continued to have great influence, particularly in the United States (plates 82 and 83), until the end of World War II.

The United States, in fact, proved to be a fertile field for most twentieth-century design innovations. The Arts and Crafts movement had a profound effect on a developing sense of design consciousness and prepared the way for such important American innovators as Louis Sullivan (1856–1924) and Frank Lloyd Wright (1867–1959).

Sullivan was primarily an architect, not a furniture designer, though he did inspire certain designs (plate 86), but his advocacy of both functionalism and the machine served as a source of inspiration to several generations of pupils, including Wright. Sullivan's statement that "ornament is mentally a luxury, not a necessity," became a byword of the Chicago School—an amorphous group of architects and designers centered in the rapidly expanding city during the late nineteenth and early twentieth centuries. The most influential among these experimenters with form and material was Wright, an early exponent of factory production and one of the very first designers to advocate and create built-in furnishings.

82

83

84

85

84.
Writing desk and side chair, oak, upholstered, designed by Frank Lloyd Wright
for the Imperial Hotel in Tokyo. American,
c. 1935, after a design of about 1920. Cooper-
Hewitt Museum, gift of Tetsuzo Inumaru

85.
Library table, oak, designed by Frank Lloyd
Wright. Though traditional in his preference for wood over metal, Wright was
distinctly modern in his taste for bold, geometric shapes. American, c. 1912–14. Metropolitan Museum of Art, New York,
purchase, Emily C. Chadbourne Bequest,
1972

86.
Dining table, carved cherry, showing in-
fluence of Louis Sullivan and Henry Hobson
Richardson (1838–1886) and attributed to
the Tobey Furniture Company of Chicago.
American, c. 1890. Metropolitan Museum of
Art, New York, gift of Mrs. Frank W. Mc-
Cabe, 1968

87.
Table, marquetry work in tulipwood, violet
wood, holly and ebony. Designed by Clark
Jones, this piece of furniture reflects a more
traditional current in American furniture design. American, 1924. Metropolitan Museum
of Art, New York, Edward C. Moore, Jr.,
Gift Fund, 1925

86

87

Born in the Wisconsin countryside, Frank Lloyd Wright had a lifelong love for wood, particularly heavily grained native timbers such as oak, and a strong belief in the unity of a structure and its furnishings. His complex, constructed furniture (plates 84 and 85) was intended mainly for residential use and reflected his interest in Japanese architecture and interiors.

Most American furniture of this period was generally of wood (plate 87) and other natural materials, but in Europe the Modern movement was rapidly expanding its vocabulary of industrial substances and incorporating them in new and exciting designs. Within a few years of Le Corbusier's establishment of the Union des Artistes Modernes, the focus of the Modern movement shifted from Germany to France and even London.

Meanwhile the National Socialists in Germany showed little sympathy for what they perceived as the "decadent" new mode. The Bauhaus was closed in 1933, and Gropius moved to England the following year. In 1937 he left for the United States, a pattern of exodus also followed by Mies van der Rohe and Marcel Breuer. While important ideas continued to be explored in France during the late 1930s, the pressures of living and working under the Nazi shadow caused more and more modernist designers to seek a haven in North America, so that by 1940 there was truly an "International style," but its practitioners were largely to be found in the New World.

Much the same may be said of Art Deco. The Paris Exposition of 1925 had had a profound effect on the American consciousness, and a wave of French imports in the "new" style was followed by local adaptations, many of them machine made, with the architectural and artistic aspects of the movement particularly emphasized. The crowning achievement of American Art Deco was the mammoth Rockefeller Center in New York, begun in 1931 and completed nine years later.

The impact of the International style in the mid-1930s, and the work of Breuer, Gropius and other expatriates, led to an interesting amalgamation of styles that some have termed *Moderne*. Featuring a combination of industrial materials such as steel and aluminum with rich woods and marbles appropriated from the Art Deco, it is best seen in the American buildings and luxury autos of the late 1930s.

Yet another branch of the International style, and one that has had a major impact on world design during the past thirty years, was centered in Scandinavia, chiefly in Denmark, Sweden and Finland. All three nations have an abundance of hardwoods, a natural love of wooden furnishings and a strong craft tradition, which was formalized, soon after 1900, in the creation of various handicraft guilds. The Scandinavian furniture designers were strongly drawn to the tenets of modernism but, for the most part, they chose to substitute plywood and springy native timbers for the steel and plastic favored elsewhere.

One of the first men to experiment in this manner was the Swede Carl Malmsten (1888–1972), who was already designing spare, practical wood and textile furniture in the 1920s (plate 88).

Other important northern designers of the period were Kaare Klint (1888–1954), an architect who headed the first class in furniture design at the Danish Royal Academy School of Architecture, and Alvar Aalto (1898–1976), a Finnish designer who adapted Breuer's steel-spring support system for use in chairs and lounges made of laminated plywood steamed and bent to fit the shape of the human body. Aalto's furniture was generally of birch—a wood he favored for its dense grain, enabling it to be shaped into many different positions, and for its lovely color (plate 89).

The end of World War II saw a general revulsion in some quarters toward the allegedly cold and unnatural quality of much contemporary furniture, and designers turned away from tubular steel, glass and plastics toward wood. It was natural, then, for the Scandinavians, who had always appreciated the strength and beauty of wood, to come to the fore. Danish and Swedish furniture had created much excitement at the 1939 New York World's Fair, and soon after 1945, a new movement, known as Scandinavian Modern, became the rage in the United States.

Built for comfort and practicality, these primarily wooden furnishings seemed to blend perfectly with postwar interiors. They triggered a whole series of hand- and factory-made imitations. The finest examples, however, were made in Denmark by such designer-craftsmen as Hans Wegner (b. 1914), Arne Jacobsen (1902–1971) and Finn Juhl (b. 1912). Wegner and Juhl were both pioneers in the Danish design movement during the 1930s, and their postwar popularity was the culmination of long and successful careers. Wegner is best known for his chairs, which incorporate a vaguely Oriental form with the employment of exposed construction as a type of decorative embellishment (colorplate 29). Juhl is equally inventive in the use of his floating device, a technique whereby the separations between chair backs and seats (plate 90) and drawers and drawer frames are emphasized to create an illusion of independence and lightness in a piece.

The Scandinavian designers did not restrict themselves solely to natural materials. Jacobsen, an architect and interior designer who had great impact on postwar styles, was a pioneer in the use of molded plastic. In 1957 he introduced two chairs in upholstered or leather-covered plastic, the "Egg" (plate 91) and the "Swan." His designs featured lightweight aluminum bases and form-fitting bodies that balanced perfectly upon them. More recently another Dane, Gunnar Aagaard Anderson, has utilized polyurethane foam to achieve equally spectacular results (plate 92).

88.
Chair, painted wood with needlework seat and back panel. Until well into this century Swedish design was still strongly Neoclassic, as may be seen in this chair by Carl Malmsten. Swedish, c. 1920. Metropolitan Museum of Art, New York, Edward C. Moore, Jr., Gift Fund, 1927

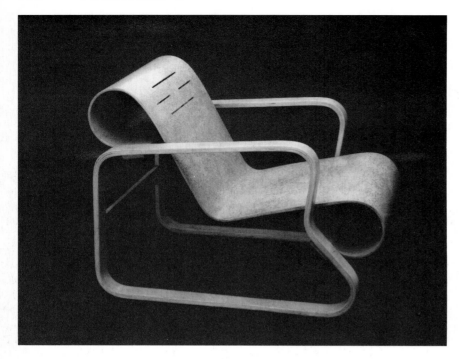

89.
Armchair, molded and bent birch plywood, designed by Alvar Aalto and manufactured by Artek Oy, Finland. Finnish, c. 1934. Museum of Modern Art, New York, gift of Edgar Kaufmann, Jr.

One Scandinavian who had an early and profound influence on American furniture design was Eero Saarinen (1910–1961), a Finn who emigrated to this country in 1923. Saarinen was among the first to see the construction possibilities inherent in plastics, and in 1946 he created the molded-plastic shell armchair. Upholstered in foam rubber and supported on a framework of tubular steel, the "womb chair," as it came to be known, proved to be a popular haven in a troubled world. In 1957 Saarinen took the process a step further by eliminating all metal and designing a pedestal chair of plastic reinforced by fiberglass (plate 93).

Saarinen's importance in American design was not dependent on his innovations alone. He was also an able teacher, including among his students Charles Eames (1907–1978), who worked for him in the late thirties. An architect and industrial designer, Eames was one of the first North American furniture designers to achieve international stature.

Eames worked in a wide variety of materials, including molded plastic and wire mesh, but his greatest affinity was for wood, particularly plywood. His most successful piece in this medium was a shock-mounted side chair consisting of molded-plywood seat and back welded to a tubular-steel frame. Nearly indestructible, this chair has become a basic piece of office furniture throughout the world. On the other hand, his light and simple all-plywood pieces (plate 94) are more aesthetically pleasing.

Colorplate 29.
Chair, walnut and mahogany with cane seat. Designed by Hans Wegner, based on an ancient Chinese prototype. Danish, 1952. Metropolitan Museum of Art, New York, Edward C. Moore, Jr., Gift Fund, 1961

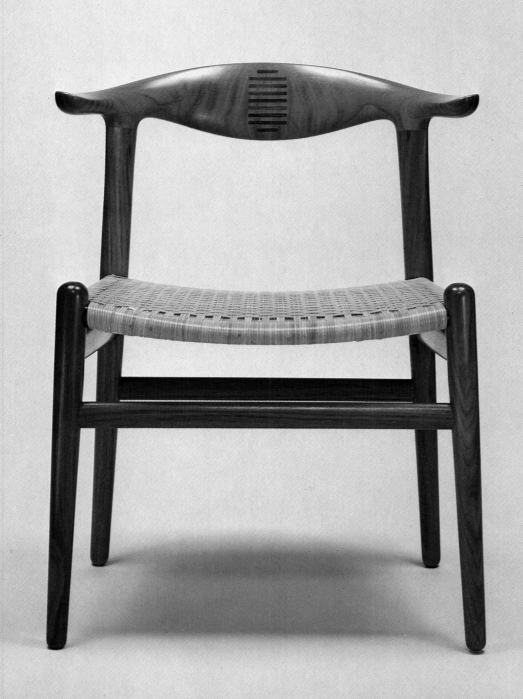

90.
Settee, framed in teak with a leather back
and seat. Designed with a "floating back" by
Finn Juhl and manufactured by Niels Vod-
der, this piece is typical of the Danish
Modern style. Danish, mid-twentieth cen-
tury. Metropolitan Museum of Art, New
York, Edward C. Moore, Jr., Gift Fund, 1961

91.
Easy chair in egg shape, plastic, oxhide and aluminum, designed by Arne Jacobsen. Danish, 1958. Metropolitan Museum of Art, New York, Edward C. Moore, Jr., Gift Fund, 1961

92

93

92.
Armchair in polyurethane foam, designed by Gunnar Aagaard Anderson. Danish, 1964. Museum of Modern Art, New York, gift of the designer

93.
Pedestal chair, molded plastic reinforced with fiberglass, designed by Eero Saarinen. American, 1957. Museum of Modern Art, New York, gift of Knoll Associates

94.
Child's chair, laminated and shaped birch. This piece was designed by Charles Eames, who is generally regarded as one of the most important native-born American contemporary furniture designers. American, 1944. Cooper-Hewitt Museum, gift of Mrs. R. Wallace Bowman

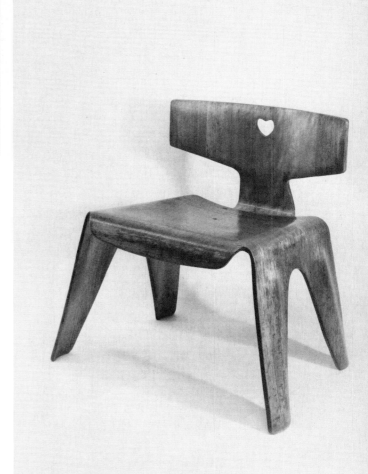

94

95.
Armchair, lacquered wood, Bakelite and chrome-steel tubing. Dutch, mid-twentieth century. Metropolitan Museum of Art, New York, Chace Foundation and Edgar Kaufmann, Jr., Gifts, 1976

96.
Lounge chair, removable nylon stretch fabric over a white fiberglass frame, designed by Pierre Paulin. French, 1968. Museum of Modern Art, New York, gift of Turner T. Ltd., New York, and Artifort, Maastricht

95

96

97

97.
Side chair, wood lacquered in black. Designed by Gilbert Rohde, this piece was manufactured by Herman Miller of Zeeland, Michigan. American, c. 1941–44. Metropolitan Museum of Art, New York, Chace Foundation and Edgar Kaufmann, Jr., Gifts, 1976

98.
Music stand, cherry, designed by Wharton Esherick. American, 1962. Metropolitan Museum of Art, New York, gift of Dr. Irwin R. Berman in memory of his father, Allan Lake Berman, 1979

Since World War II the International style has continued to dominate Western design in both form and use of materials. The Scandinavian preference for wood has been more than matched by tremendous strides in the employment of synthetics—chair shells of compressed, molded fiberglass; woven fabric coverings of Orlon, nylon and rayon; vinyl and other coated fabrics that look and feel like wool or leather; rubberized upholstery hair; hinges and other "hardware" of nylons that have proved stronger and quieter in use than metal.

Designers in both Europe and the United States have used these materials well in creating light and durable but stylish furnishings available at all price levels: built-in furniture, modular pieces that can be arranged and rearranged to suit one's taste or circumstances, stacking chairs and tables for the modern, small apartment—the list goes on and on. In Europe, the Dutch (plate 95) and the Italians (colorplate 30) have been active; but perhaps the most inventive pieces have come from Scandinavia and from France, where designers like Pierre Paulin have made major strides in combining nylon and fiberglass (plate 96).

In the United States, a similar interest in synthetics has been balanced by a strong movement toward the employment of wood. This has been evident in Eames's work and that of Gilbert Rohde (1894–1944) (plate 97). Another enthusiast for the natural medium was Wharton Esherick (1887–1970), who trained as a woodworker and whose later creations relied for their effect on the grain and natural formation of the pieces of wood from which they were made (plate 98).

Given the strong and continuing interest in furniture design both in the United States and abroad, there seems little doubt that the International style's practitioners will continue to provide attractive and practical furnishings for generations to come. The proposition that form follows function will also remain, in the foreseeable future, the byword of furniture design throughout the Western world.

98

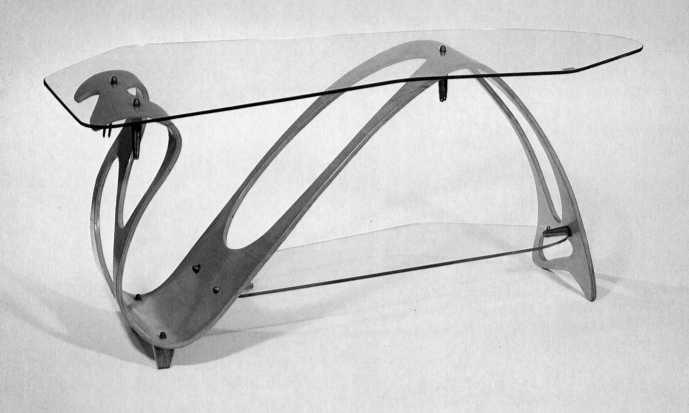

7   Advice for the Collector

The would-be collector of 1800–1950 furniture faces an intriguing yet complex set of choices. In this relatively brief time span more furniture pieces of greater variety and from a more varied range of materials have been produced than in all of previous history. This bewildering variety offers great opportunities for the collector, but it also requires more in the way of expertise.

On the one hand, collectors, particularly those interested in Victorian or Neoclassic examples, must be aware of all the admonitions as to restoration, repair and outright reproduction set out in Chapter 7 of *Furniture 1*. On the other hand, the anonymous nature of much late Victorian and twentieth-century furniture requires a highly developed sense of taste as well as the ability to judge condition and authenticity.

Experience and knowledge, which come only from time spent looking at the pieces available in museum and private collections, are always important. It is vital to be able to distinguish the patina and feel of old wood, to be able to recognize hand-formed nails, screws and hinges and to know styles well enough to be able to spot a "marriage" between two mismatched portions of a highboy or table.

Taste is something else again. During the late 1800s furniture factories turned out vast quantities of walnut and rosewood furnishings in the popular rococo and Renaissance revival styles. In the early twentieth century many manufacturers made what was termed Mission-style furniture. Most of the former lacked the flair and quality of workmanship found in pieces by Belter and Meeks; most of the latter failed to achieve the classic simplicity and honesty of construction inherent in a Stickley chair or a Roycroft table. The ability to recognize the better examples on their form alone is not possessed by everyone. It is possible to know a great deal about how furniture is

Colorplate 30.
Tea table, maple, plywood and glass. Designed by Carlo Mollino and made in Turin by Apelli and Varesio, this piece has a fluidity reminiscent of Art Nouveau. Italian, c. 1950. Brooklyn Museum, New York, gift of the Italian Government

put together and be able to distinguish one stylistic period from another but still to lack the knack of choosing those examples whose form sets them off as superior.

The problem continues into this century. Breuer's tubular-steel armchair and Mies van der Rohe's cantilever suspension system were major innovations in furniture design, and they have been mimicked by dozens of other designers, not always successfully. Distinguishing previously unrecognized examples by designers and manufacturers who were not acknowledged during their day is like treasure hunting, and has the same rewards and pitfalls.

Still, there is a wonderful world of collecting awaiting those who are willing to educate their judgment and to seek out the best of contemporary furnishings. Such pieces, which can be purchased today as furnishings, may in the future be collected as works of craft-art and, eventually, as valued antiques. Of course, such purchases are gambles; not every designer is a Le Corbusier, and most of the work being done today will sink into obscurity. But certain pieces and the work of certain artists will remain; and those who have had the judgment to seek them out will be rewarded by both an increase in monetary value and the satisfaction of knowing that they have preserved something beautiful for the generations of collectors to come.

And preservation is important, even with the seemingly indestructible steel and plastic of which so many contemporary examples are made. Modern-day collectors of furniture will have to know as much about the upkeep of polyurethanes, synthetic fabrics and chrome as those interested in earlier pieces must know about wood, natural fabrics and lacquers. In each case preservation of the object in its original state will take care and understanding.

Glossary

Bakelite, a trademarked term referring to various thermosetting resins or plastics used in making furniture mounts and household accessories. Bakelite knobs and pulls are often seen on mass-produced furniture in the Art Deco mode.

block front, the front of a case piece carved in three parts, with the center section either extended beyond or recessed behind the side sections.

boss, a knoblike, projecting ornament, usually found on chests.

bun foot, a slightly flattened, round foot.

burl, a protruding, irregularly grained growth on a tree. It is often used in thinly sliced sections as veneer.

cabriole leg, a reverse-curved leg ending in a shaped foot.

cane, an East Indian climbing palm whose stems are used to manufacture lightweight furniture and, split, as seating material.

cantilever, a form of modern furniture suspension usually featuring a bracket-shaped base that supports other elements of a chair or settee. Mies van der Rohe is generally credited with applying the cantilever principle to furniture design.

celluloid, one of the earliest plastics, sometimes used in the making of early twentieth-century furniture.

chip carving, shallow decorative carving executed with a chisel and generally composed of geometrical patterns. A medieval technique, it was revived in the late nineteenth century.

chrome, metal plated with an alloy of the element chromium and having a shiny, silverlike appearance. Chrome steel is much favored by modern designers.

cloisonné, the technique of covering an object's surface with vitrified enamels separated by metal strips so as to create a design.

C-scroll, a scroll carved in the form of the letter C.

dovetail, a right-angled joint formed by interlocking tenons resembling the shape of a dove's tail.

dowel, a wooden pin or peg used to join two pieces of wood.

ebonized, wood that has been stained or painted black in imitation of the rare and costly ebony wood. Ebonized finishes were common during the Empire and Victorian periods and are still employed.

fall front, the writing board of a desk, which falls forward to form the writing surface.

fiberglass, glass in a fibrous form, often used in contemporary furniture design and in textiles.

finial, a terminal ornament. In American furniture, most often in the form of an urn or a pineapple.

gilt, a thin layer of gold or something simulating it.

gilt bronze, gilded bronze used in furniture decoration. Gilt-bronze fixtures were most common during the Empire era, though they have been employed at other times as well.

inlay, decoration formed by contrasting materials, or materials of contrasting color, set into the surface of a piece.

intarsia, a form of inlay in multicolored woods often used to decorate furniture.

lacquer, spirit varnish applied in many layers on a wood surface to build up a hard, highly polished surface.

lamination, the bonding together under heat and pressure of thin sheets of wood. Glue or resin is employed as a bonding agent; usually, the sheets are set at an angle to each other. See *plywood*.

leatherette, a plastic or paper composition that is colored and embossed to look like leather. Often used in mass-produced twentieth-century furnishings.

marquetry, inlay of thinly sliced materials such as wood, ivory, bone, metal or mother-of-pearl into a background of veneer.

monopodium, a support derived from an ancient design, consisting of an animal leg surmounted by an animal head.

pad foot, the simple flattish end of a cabriole leg.

palisander, a Brazilian rosewood that was popular in the nineteenth century as well as with Art Deco designers.

patent furniture, a term used in reference to the mechanical and semimechanical pieces made in great numbers during the nineteenth century. Many such pieces were never really patented.

Pembroke table, a small, rectangular, drop-leaf table, usually with straight legs.

plywood, sheets of laminated wood in which the grain of each sheet lies at right angles to those next to it. Extremely strong and flexible.

polyurethanes, a variety of synthetic substances that can serve in rigid or flexible form as substitutes for natural substances used in furniture design.

revealed construction, furniture design in which structural components such as joints, nails and dovetails are employed as decorative elements rather than being concealed as was the custom during the Victorian and to some extent the modern eras.

secondary woods, inexpensive or imperfect woods used for drawer linings, backs and carcasses of case pieces and other structural elements not readily visible.

secretary, a desk, usually slant-top, with a bookcase above.

settee, a seat with back and arms large enough for two.

settle, a long seat with a high or low closed back and solid wood ends.

shagreen, treated sharkskin or leather, a material favored by Art Deco designers.

S-scroll, a scroll in the form of the letter S.

strapwork, flat, interlaced bands applied or carved on a surface.

stretch fabrics, artificial or natural fabrics elastic in nature, allowing them to be stretched over a furniture frame to provide a smooth, skin-tight covering.

synthetics, artificial materials (such as plastic) and man-made textiles that are widely used in contemporary furnishings to fill the role once assigned to natural components like wood and cotton.

tambour front, a term referring to small, horizontal sliding doors often seen on desks that consist of narrow strips of wood glued to a flexible canvas backing so they can be rolled into a recess to provide access to storage space. Forerunner of the familiar rolltop desk.

tubular steel, thin sheets of steel rolled into a hollow tube to produce a lightweight and flexible furniture-making material. Tubular steel is one of the most important twentieth-century furniture components.

turning, a way of forming columnar-shaped members of chairs, tables and cupboards by means of a revolving lathe.

vellum, fine-grained, unsplit lamb- or calfskin used in book binding and furniture making.

veneer, a thin layer of decorative material glued to a thicker backing.

verre églomisé, glass painted on the reverse, used as decorative inserts on furniture.

Reading and Reference

General

ARONSON, JOSEPH. *The Encyclopedia of Furniture.* 3rd ed., rev. New York: Crown Publishers, 1965.

ASLIN, ELIZABETH. *Nineteenth-Century English Furniture.* New York: T. Yoseloff, 1962.

BISHOP, ROBERT, AND PATRICIA COBLENTZ. *The World of Antiques: Art and Architecture in Victorian America.* New York: E. P. Dutton and Co., 1979.

BOGER, LOUISE A., AND H. BATTERSON. *The Dictionary of Antiques and the Decorative Arts.* New York: Charles Scribner's Sons, 1967.

BRIDGMAN, HARRIET, AND ELIZABETH DRURY, EDS. *The Encyclopedia of Victoriana,* New York: Macmillan Co., 1975.

COMSTOCK, HELEN. *American Furniture: Seventeenth, Eighteenth, and Nineteenth Century Styles.* New York: Viking Press, 1962.

CORNELIUS, CHARLES O. *Furniture Masterpieces of Duncan Phyfe.* 1922. Reprint. New York: Dover Publications, 1970.

FLEMING, JOHN, AND HUGH HONOUR, *Dictionary of the Decorative Arts.* New York: Harper & Row, 1977.

GLOAG, JOHN. *A Social History of Furniture Design from B.C. 1300 to A.D. 1960.* New York, Crown Publishers, 1966.

GRANDJEAN, SERGE. *Empire Furniture: 1800–1825.* New York: Taplinger, 1966.

HAYWARD, HELEN, ED. *World Furniture.* New York: McGraw-Hill Book Co., 1965.

HILLIER, BEVIS. *Art Deco.* New York: E. P. Dutton and Co., 1968.

HIMMELHEBER, GEORG. *Biedermeier Furniture.* Translated and edited by Simon Jervis. London: Faber and Faber, 1974.

HINCKLEY, F. LEWIS. *A Dictionary of Antique Furniture.* New York: Crown Publishers, 1953.

JOY, EDWARD T. *The Book of English Furniture.* South Brunswick, N.J.: A. S. Barnes & Co., 1966.

———. *The Connoisseur Illustrated Guides: Furniture.* New York: Hearst Books, 1972.

KETCHUM, WILLIAM C. *The Family Treasury of Antiques.* New York: A & W Publishers, 1978.

LESIEUTRE, ALAIN. *The Spirit and Splendour of Art Deco.* New York: Paddington Press, 1974.

METROPOLITAN MUSEUM OF ART. *Nineteenth-Century America: Furniture and Other Decorative Arts.* New York: New York Graphic Society, 1971.

ORMSBEE, THOMAS H. *Field Guide to American Victorian Furniture.* New York: Bonanza Books, 1952.

PEHNT, WOLFGANG, ED. *Encyclopedia of Modern Architecture.* New York: Harry N. Abrams, 1964.

PEVSNER, NIKOLAUS. *Pioneers of Modern Design: From William Morris to Walter Gropius.* New York: Museum of Modern Art, 1949.

PHILLIPS, PHOEBE, ED. *The Collectors' Encyclopedia of Antiques.* New York: Crown Publishers, 1973.

ZAHLE, ERIK, ED. *A Treasury of Scandinavian Design.* New York: Golden Press, 1961.

Catalogues

McFADDEN, DAVID R. *Furniture in the Collection of the Cooper-Hewitt Museum.* New York: Cooper-Hewitt Museum, Smithsonian Institution, 1979.

The Metropolitan Museum of Art Bulletin, XXXVII, no. 3 (1979/80).

Some Public Collections of Furniture

Index

Acknowledgments

Cooper-Hewitt staff members have been responsible for the following contributions to the series: concept, Lisa Taylor; administration, Christian Rohlfing, David McFadden and Kurt Struver; coordination, Peter Scherer. In addition, valuable help has been provided by S. Dillon Ripley, Joseph Bonsignore, Susan Hamilton and Robert W. Mason of the Smithsonian Institution, as well as by the late Warren Lynch, Gloria Norris and Edward E. Fitzgerald of Book-of-the-Month Club, Inc.

The author wishes to thank the following for their kind assistance: Brenda Gilchrist, whose patience, knowledge and good humor made the rough spots smooth; David Hanks, David McFadden and Christian Rohlfing, whose comments on the text were of great help; and Ann Adelman, Joan Hoffman, Neal Jones and Peter Scherer.

Credits

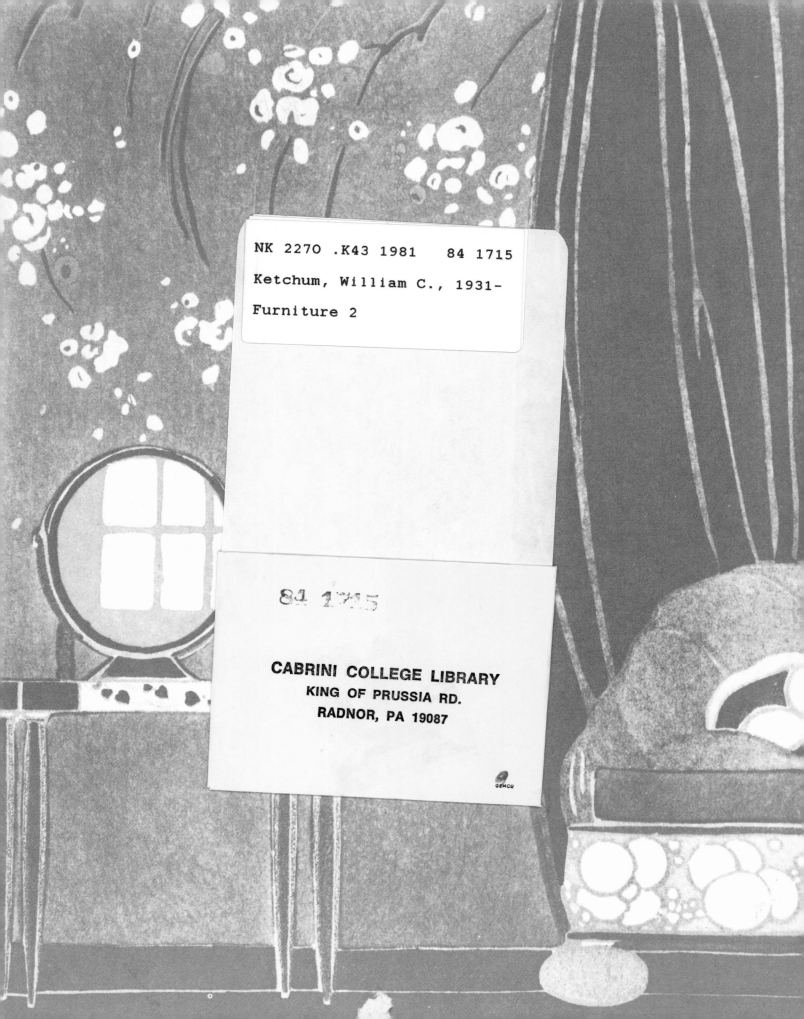